Study Guide for
Practical Statistics
for Educators

Fourth Edition

Study Guide for
Practical Statistics for Educators

Fourth Edition

Ruth Ravid
and
Elizabeth Oyer

ROWMAN & LITTLEFIELD PUBLISHERS, INC.
Lanham • Boulder • New York • Toronto • Plymouth, UK

Published by Rowman & Littlefield Publishers, Inc.
A wholly owned subsidiary of The Rowman & Littlefield Publishing Group, Inc.
4501 Forbes Boulevard, Suite 200, Lanham, Maryland 20706
http://www.rowmanlittlefield.com

Estover Road, Plymouth PL6 7PY, United Kingdom

British Library Cataloguing in Publication Information Available

Library of Congress Cataloging-in-Publication Data
Ravid, Ruth.
  Study guide for practical statistics for educators / Ruth Ravid and Elizabeth Oyer. — 4th ed.
    p. cm.
  Companion to: Practical statistics for educators.
  Includes index.
  ISBN 978-1-4422-0845-2 (pbk. : alk. paper) — ISBN 978-1-4422-0846-9 (electronic)
  1. Educational statistics—Study and teaching. 2. Educational tests and measurements.
I. Oyer, Elizabeth, 1970– II. Ravid, Ruth. Practical statistics for educators. III. Title.
  LB2846.R333 2011
  370.2'1—dc22   2011008096

∞™ The paper used in this publication meets the minimum requirements of
American National Standard for Information Sciences—Permanence of Paper for
Printed Library Materials, ANSI/NISO Z39.48-1992.

Printed in the United States of America

Contents

Preface

This study guide accompanies the textbook PRACTICAL STATISTICS FOR EDUCATORS (4th ed., Ravid, 2010). The main purpose of the study guide is to allow students to review and apply the material presented in the textbook. The chapters and exercises in the study guide correspond to the chapters in the textbook. The study guide includes exercises that require students to recall, comprehend, apply, interpret, analyze, and synthesize information. Various item formats are used, such as multiple-choice, matching, filling-in-the-blanks, short answers, and computation. Answers to each chapter's exercises can be found at the end of the chapter to allow students to get immediate feedback and confirm their own answers. The answers to some of the exercises include detailed explanations of the correct answers in order to elaborate on the reasons for the correct response.

Because more and more people use statistical software programs to analyze their data, the study guide includes only a few exercises that require the use of calculators. The emphasis is on skills that every teacher researcher needs to know: How to select the appropriate statistical test to analyze the data and how to interpret the data calculated by the computer. Supplemental computer exercises that apply the chapter content are at the end of many chapters. The exercises require the use of Microsoft™ Office Excel, version 1997 or later.[1] Technical tips provided are for Microsoft™ Office Excel, version 2007. The data required for the exercises are available for download at http://www.evalsolutions.net/portal/studyguide. The username for the site is *studyguide*, and the password is *practical10*.

NOTE

1. Microsoft Office Excel is a registered trademark of Microsoft Corporation. Screen shots are reproduced with the permission of Microsoft Corporation and are not intended to suggest an endorsement of this study guide.

1

An Overview of Educational Research

Circle the correct answer between the choices in bold:

1.1. The type of research designed to solve a problem by studying it and implementing a solution to the problem is called **basic / action** research

1.2. The type of research where researchers focus on studying a limited number of cases in their natural context, using multiple and subjective data sources is called **qualitative / quantitative** research.

1.3. In experimental studies, researchers manipulate the **dependent / independent** variable and observe its effect on the **dependent / independent** variable.

1.4. In causal-comparative studies, the independent variable **is / is not** manipulated.

1.5. In experimental studies, unplanned or uncontrolled variables which may affect the outcomes of the studies are called **dependent / extraneous** variables.

1.6. Studies in which extraneous variables are controlled are said to have high **internal / external** validity.

1.7. When the results of the study can be generalized to other settings and populations, the study is considered to have **independent / external** validity.

1.8. In studies where people behave in a way that is different from their normal behavior because they are being observed by the researchers, there may be a threat to the study's **statistical regression / external validity**.

1.9. In most experimental studies, when the groups being compared are formed by randomly assigning people to groups, these groups are considered **more / less** similar to each other compared with the majority of studies where intact groups are being compared.

1.10. In pre-experimental studies, there is usually a **greater / smaller** number of threats to internal validity compared with true experimental studies.

1.11. Experimental and control groups are tested *repeatedly* before and after the intervention in quasi-experimental studies which are called **time-series / counterbalanced** designs.

1.12. In studies where a counterbalanced design is used, all groups receive all interventions in **the same / a different** order.

1.13. A-B-A designs are used to study the effect of an intervention on **individuals / groups**.

1.14. A-B-A designs include **one / two** baseline phase(s) and **one / two** intervention phase(s).

1.15. Studies designed to measure how children change over time, without the use of any planned intervention, are called **cross-sectional / time-series** studies.

Circle the best answer:

1.16. The type of research which is aimed at testing theories and applying them to specific situations is called _____

    a. applied research.
    b. action research.
    c. pure research.
    d. basic research.

1.17. Research conducted in the lab under a tight control of all variables is called _____

    a. applied research.
    b. action research.
    c. basic research.
    d. qualitative research.

1.18. Studies where researchers look for changes in the dependent variable which may happen as a result of their manipulation of the independent variable are called _____ studies.

    a. experimental
    b. ex post facto
    c. causal-comparative
    d. qualitative

1.19. Studies which focus on establishing a cause-and-effect relationship are called _____

    a. qualitative studies.
    b. descriptive studies.
    c. experimental studies.
    d. cross-sectional studies.

1.20. Uncontrolled events happening outside longer-duration experimental studies which can have an effect on the dependent variable, may pose a threat to the study's internal validity that is called _____

    a. instrumentation.
    b. statistical regression.
    c. testing.
    d. history.

1.21. Causal-comparative research is also called _____

    a. pre-experimental research.
    b. ex-post facto research.
    c. action research.
    d. time-series research.

1.22. Experimental studies where two pre-existing groups are used as experimental and control groups are called _____

    a. true experimental studies.
    b. cross-sectional studies.
    c. quasi-experimental design studies.
    d. A-B-A case studies.

1.23. To study how individuals change over time, researchers may conduct _____

    a. causal-comparative research.
    b. true experimental research.
    c. time-series research.
    d. cross-sectional research.

1.24. Studies where data are collected over two or more points in time for the *same* people are called _____

    a. cross-sectional studies.
    b. panel studies.
    c. trend studies.
    d. case studies.

1.25. A study is designed to assess the effect of cooperative learning on the social skills of third-grade students. Twice a day, during free play, observers count the number of positive interactions among the students who are taught using cooperative learning. In this study, the *independent* variable is the _____

    a. cooperative learning.
    b. students' grade level.
    c. number of positive interactions.
    d. number of free play periods during the day.

1.26. A study is designed to assess whether technology training is likely to increase teachers' use of instructional technology in their teaching. Teachers who have participated in 10-day technology training in the use of various instructional technologies are observed for three months before and after the training to determine how many hours per week they use instructional technology in their teaching. In this study, the *dependent* variable is the _____

    a. semester-long instructional technology training course.
    b. number of hours per week that teachers use instructional technology in their teaching.
    c. training of the observers who record teachers' technology use in the classrooms.
    d. periods of three months before and after the study, when teachers are observed.

1.27. A school psychologist wants to conduct a causal-comparative study to explore the effect of grade level on the self-concept of middle-school students. The psychologist administers a measure of self-concept to a group of 300 students from grades 6, 7, and 8, and compares the self-concept mean scores of students in the three grade levels. In this study, the *independent* variable is the _____

    a. school psychologist.
    b. number of students.
    c. students' grade levels.
    d. students' self-concept scores.

1.28. The study described in the previous question (question #1.27, about grade level and self-concept) is considered a causal-comparative study because _____

    a. the dependent variable cannot be manipulated.
    b. the independent variable cannot be manipulated.
    c. there are three different grade levels in the study.
    d. some extraneous variables cannot be controlled in this study.

1.29. A third-grade social studies teacher started to use differentiated instruction this year for the first time with her English Language Learners (ELLs). The teacher measures her students' scores on the district's end-of-year social studies test for third graders and compares these scores to those obtained on the same test by similar ELLs from the previous year who were not taught using differentiated instruction. In this study, the *independent* variable is the _____

    a. English language learners.
    b. time of year the test is given.
    c. the new teaching method - differentiated instruction.
    d. students' scores on the district's social studies end-of-year test.

1.30. A study is conducted to test two methods to treat depressed teenagers. Seventy children, ages 13–18, diagnosed as depressed, are randomly assigned to the two intervention groups. The two interventions consist of a series of weekly meetings and online chats among the members of each group and their counselors. A measure to assess their level of depression is administered to the study's participants before and after the intervention. The design of the study is _____

    a. true experimental design.
    b. counterbalanced design.
    c. quasi-experimental design.
    d. time-series design.

CHAPTER 1 ANSWERS

(1.1)   action. (Explanation: Basic research is conducted in highly controlled settings and is designed to develop theories and generalities without an attempt to solve an immediate problem, whereas action research is conducted to solve a specific problem in a particular context.)

(1.2)   qualitative. (Explanation: Qualitative research is conducted with a small number of cases in their natural environment using multiple data sources. Quantitative research is often conducted to study cause-and-effect relationship or to describe existing situations and relationships among numerical variables.)

(1.3)   independent; dependent. (Explanation: The independent variable in experimental studies is the intervention or treatment which is manipulated and controlled by the researcher. The outcome variable [e.g., post-test] is the dependent variable.)

(1.4)   is not. (Explanation: In causal-comparative studies the independent variable cannot be manipulated because it has already occurred by the time the study starts; or it cannot or should not be manipulated.)

(1.5)   extraneous. (Explanation: Extraneous variables refer to other plausible explanations that can impact the study in addition to the independent variable being studied. Dependent variables are the outcome variables and are not manipulated.)

(1.6)   internal. (Explanation: Internal validity is achieved when the extraneous variables are being controlled.)

(1.7)   external. (Explanation: External validity refers to the extent to which the results of the study can be generalized to other settings.)

(1.8)   external validity. (Explanation: The phenomenon of people behaving differently when they perceive they are being studied is a common threat to the study's external validity. Statistical regression is a threat to the study's internal validity.)

(1.9)   more. (Explanation: Groups formed by using random assignment are considered to be more similar to each other compared with groups formed by using any other procedure.)

(1.10)   greater. (Explanation: In pre-experimental designs it is more difficult to control variables that may negatively affect the study's internal validity.)

(1.11)   time-series. (Explanation: In time-series designs, there is usually only one intervention, and the groups are tested several times before and after the intervention; in counterbalanced designs, there are several interventions, but only one testing after each intervention.)

(1.12)   a different. (Explanation: The interventions are applied to the groups in different order to ensure that the order of the intervention does not pose a threat to the study's internal validity.)

(1.13)   individuals. (Explanation: The A-B-A designs are typical of experimental studies where individuals are used as their own control.)

(1.14)   two; one. (Explanation: The letter A refers to the baseline phase and B is the intervention phase; therefore, in A-B-A designs there are two baseline phases and one intervention phase.)

(1.15)   cross-sectional. (Explanation: Cross-sectional designs are used in nonexperimental studies, while time-series designs include interventions.)

(1.16)   a. (Explanation: The purpose of applied research is to test theories in specific situations.)

(1.17)   c. (Explanation: Pure [i.e., basic] research is conducted in labs under tight control whereas the other types of research are done in real-life situations.)

(1.18)   a. (Explanation: In causal-comparative / ex post facto studies and in qualitative research studies, the independent variable is not manipulated at all; it is manipulated only in experimental studies.)

(1.19)   c. (Explanation: Only well-designed experimental studies can establish cause-and-effect relationship with a high degree of confidence.)

(1.20) d. (Explanation: History can pose a threat to the study's internal validity in studies of longer duration where events that happen outside the study can impact the outcome variable [i.e., dependent variable].)

(1.21) b. (Explanation: *Ex post facto*, which means "after the fact," is often used interchangeably with the term *causal comparative*. Both refer to studies that investigate cause-and-effect relationship without manipulating the independent variable.)

(1.22) c. (Explanation: In quasi-experimental designs, pre-existing groups are being compared; by comparison, in true experimental studies, participants are randomly assigned to groups.)

(1.23) d. (Explanation: Cross-sectional studies include similar groups of people of different ages with the assumption that the older sample would provide an accurate picture of the younger sample a few years later.)

(1.24) b. (Explanation: In a panel study, which is considered a longitudinal study, the same group of people are followed over time.)

(1.25) a. (Explanation: This is an experimental study, designed to study cause-and-effect relationship. In the study, cooperative learning is the independent variable [the "cause"] and social skills, expressed as the number of positive interactions among the students, are the dependent variable [the "effect"].)

(1.26) b. (Explanation: The outcome measure - the dependent variable - is the teachers' use of instructional technology, expressed as the number of hours per week they use instructional technology in their teaching.)

(1.27) d. (Explanation: The school psychologist wants to test the effect of grade level on self-concept; therefore, in this causal comparative study, the students' grade level is the independent variable—the "cause"—and the students' self-concept scores are the dependent variable—the "effect.")

(1.28) b. (Explanation: In this causal-comparative study, the school psychologist cannot manipulate the independent variable of grade level. In other words, the school psychologist cannot assign students to be in a certain grade level for the purpose of the study. The dependent variable is students' self concept.)

(1.29) c. (Explanation: This is an experimental study designed to test the efficacy of using differentiated instruction with ELLs in social studies. The new teaching method is the intervention; that is, the independent variable. The dependent variable is students' scores on the district's end-of-year social studies test.)

(1.30) a. (Explanation: It is a true experimental design, because children are assigned at random to the two groups. The designs listed in the other three answers [b, c, and d] do not include groups with random assignment of participants.)

2

Basic Concepts in Statistics

Identify each as a *variable* or a *constant*:

2.1.   The *number of months* in a year.

2.2.   The *gender* of teenage girls in a study designed to investigate their career aspirations.

2.3.   The *age* when people choose to retire.

Identify each variable as *continuous* or *discrete*:

2.4.   Grade level

2.5.   Age

2.6.   Number of children in a family

Identify each as *nominal, ordinal, interval,* or *ratio*:

2.7.   The TV channel watched the most on Thursday night in four cities.

2.8.   The percentage of respondents watching each TV program at 8:00 pm on Thursday.

2.9.   The list of ACT scores for the high schools in the county.

2.10. The classification of students by the state where they were born.

2.11. The number of residents in six different states.

2.12. The ranking of a high school in a list ranking all high schools in the state.

Classify each as *descriptive* or *inferential* statistics:

2.13. The mean scores of all third grade classes on a standardized achievement test.

2.14. The TV ratings as obtained by a TV rating company for 5000 households with "people-meter" devices.

2.15. The blood pressure readings of volunteers given a new experimental drug to lower their blood pressure.

Circle the correct answer between the choices in bold:

2.16. When every 20th person is chosen from a group of 1000 people, we obtain a **systematic / random** sample.

2.17. A hypothesis that predicts that *there is* a difference or relationship between variables or groups is called the **null / alternative** hypothesis, and is represented by the symbol H_A or H_1.

2.18. In order to decide whether the null hypothesis should be rejected or retained, the *sample* statistic obtained as a result of the statistical calculations is compared to the appropriate **critical values / degrees of freedom.**

2.19. A biased sample contains a **random / systematic** error.

2.20. A random sample **is always / may not always be** representative of the population from which it was selected.

2.21. To analyze data measured on a *nominal* scale, researchers should use **parametric / nonparametric** statistics.

2.22. The information gained about the sample is used to generalize to the population and to estimate its values in **descriptive / inferential** statistics.

2.23. Inferential statistics **may / may not** include descriptive statistics, such as the mean.

2.24. When we predict which mean is going to be higher, our hypothesis is **directional / nondirectional.**

2.25. If we reject the null hypothesis at $p < .01$, we are **more / less** confident that we made the right decision compared with rejecting the null hypothesis at the $p < .05$ level.

2.26. When there is a *very small* difference between two means obtained on a measure at the end of a study, the null hypothesis is likely to be **rejected / retained.**

2.27. A low correlation is more likely to be statistically significant when the sample size is **large / small.**

2.28. When the probability level is set prior to the start of the study, it is represented by the letter p / **alpha** (α).

2.29. The error made by researchers who retain a null hypothesis when in fact it should be rejected is called **type I / type II** error.

2.30. The hypothesis that *always* states that the correlation is not significantly different from zero is the **null / alternative** hypothesis.

2.31. Effect size is used to evaluate the **practical / statistical** significance of the study.

2.32. When selecting a number of equal-size samples from the same population, the means of the samples are likely to be **the same as / different from** the population mean.

2.33. The standard error of the means is the standard deviation of the **sample means / population means.**

2.34. To estimate a population value that is of interest to them, researchers use the **effect size / confidence interval.**

Circle the best answer:

2.35. Equal distances between the various points on the scale are found in _____

    a. a nominal scale.
    b. an ordinal scale.
    c. both nominal and ordinal scales.
    d. both interval and ratio scales.

2.36. Using numbers to represent *categories* of observations is an example of a(n) _____ scale.

    a. nominal
    b. ordinal
    c. interval
    d. ratio

2.37. Equal distances between the various points on the scale, as well as an absolute zero, are found in a(n) _____ scale.

    a. nominal
    b. ordinal
    c. interval
    d. ratio

2.38. A sampling procedure where every member of the population has an independent and equal chance of being selected is called a _____ sample.

  a. systematic
  b. random
  c. stratified
  d. convenience

2.39. A sample that represents proportionally each segment of the population is a _____ sample.

  a. random
  b. systematic
  c. stratified
  d. convenient

2.40. When every 15th person is selected from a population of 2000 people, the obtained sample is a _____ sample.

  a. stratified
  b. systematic
  c. random
  d. biased

CHAPTER 2 ANSWERS

(2.1)   constant. (Explanation: The number of months is always the same: 12.)

(2.2)   constant. (Explanation: Since only girls participate, gender does not vary and is a constant.)

(2.3)   variable. (Explanation: Different people choose to retire at different ages.)

(2.4)   discrete. (Explanation: Grade levels have increments of whole units only; for example, one cannot be in grade 3.2 or in grade 11.7.)

(2.5)   continuous. (Explanation: There are many small increments between the various ages; for example, between the age of 10 and 11, there can be small increments, such as 10 years and one day, 10 years and 2 days, etc.)

(2.6)   discrete. (Explanation: The number of children is increased in whole unit's increments. Therefore, we cannot have, for example, 2.4 children in the family, only 2 or 3.)

(2.7)   nominal. (Explanation: Although the channels are represented by numbers, these numbers are used for identification only and represent categories.)

(2.8)   ratio. (Explanation: Percentages are considered a ratio scale, because "0%" is viewed as a true / absolute zero.)

(2.9)   interval. (Explanation: ACT scores, as well as most other test scores, are considered an interval scale.)

(2.10)   nominal. (Explanation: The states are categorical data.)

(2.11)   ratio. (Explanation: The number of residents in each state is likely to be different. For example, we can say that one state has twice as many people as another state.)

(2.12)   ordinal. (Explanation: By ranking observations we create an ordinal scale.)

(2.13)   descriptive. (Explanation: Since *all* the third grade classes are included, the mean is viewed as representing a population, not a sample.)

(2.14)   inferential. (Explanation: The 5000 households are considered a sample that represents the total population of TV viewers.)

(2.15)   inferential. (Explanation: The volunteers are used as a sample, and their reaction to the drug would be generalized to the general population.)

(2.16)   systematic. (Explanation: In systematic samples, every Kth person or case [e.g., every 20th person, in our example] is selected from a list of all potential participants.)

(2.17)   alternative (or *research hypothesis*). (Explanation: The null hypothesis, represented by H_0, predicts that there would be no differences between means or no correlation between variables.)

(2.18)   critical value. (Explanation: The obtained statistical value is compared to the critical value to determine whether the results are statistically significant.)

(2.19)   systematic. (Explanation: *Random* errors are expected when drawing samples from a population, but *systematic* errors in the samples indicate a bias.)

(2.20)   may not always be. (Explanation: While a random sample is likely to be representative of the population, if the sample is small [n < 30], it may not be representative of the population from which it was selected.)

(2.21)   nonparametric. (Explanation: To use *parametric* statistics, data have to be measured on an *interval* or *ratio* scale.)

(2.22)   inferential. (Explanation: Inferential statistics refer to the use of samples to estimate and make inferences about the population values.)

(2.23)   may. (Explanation: Inferential statistics may include descriptive statistics, such as the mean. The two types of statistics are not mutually exclusive.)

(2.24) directional. (Explanation: Directional hypotheses are used when the researcher predicts which mean will be higher or when the researcher predicts the direction of the correlation [positive or negative].)

(2.25) more. (Explanation: A p value of .01 indicates that there is 1% chance that the decision to reject the null hypothesis is the wrong decision, whereas a p value of .05 indicates that the likelihood is 5%. Therefore, rejecting the null hypothesis at $p < .01$ indicates more confidence in the findings than when rejecting the null hypothesis at $p < .05$.)

(2.26) retained. (Explanation: In studies where there is a small difference between the means, we are more likely to conclude that the difference could have happened purely by chance and therefore we would retain the null hypothesis.)

(2.27) large. (Explanation: When the sample sizes are large, even small correlation coefficients are likely to be statistically significant.)

(2.28) alpha (α). (Explanation: Probability levels stated prior to the start of the study are called alpha, whereas the probability levels used when analyzing the data at the end of the study are called p values.)

(2.29) type II. (Explanation: Retaining a *false* null hypothesis is referred to as Type II error, while rejecting a *true* null hypothesis is referred to as Type I error.)

(2.30) null. (Explanation: Only null hypotheses always predict that the correlation is zero. Alternative hypotheses may also predict that the correlation is positive or negative or different from zero.)

(2.31) practical. (Explanation: The p value is used to indicate the study's *statistical* significance whereas effect size is used to evaluate the *practical* significance of the results.)

(2.32) different from. (Explanation: Empirical data indicate that there is likely to be some variation in the sample statistics compared with the population from which the samples are selected, which have fixed values.)

(2.33) sample means. (Explanation: The standard error of the means is the standard deviation of the distribution of the means of equal-size samples that are selected from a given population.)

(2.34) confidence interval. (Explanation: Confidence intervals is used to estimate the range of the population values. Effect size is used to evaluate the practical significance of the results, not to predict the population values.)

(2.35) d.

(2.36) a.

(2.37) d.

(2.38) b.

(2.39) c.

(2.40) b.

Organizing and Graphing Data

Circle the correct answer between the choices in bold:

3.1. Class intervals are usually created when the range of the scores is **high / low.**

3.2. Tables that are used to indicate the number of scores at or above a given score are called **class intervals / cumulative frequencies** tables.

3.3. A graph where each bar represents a discrete and independent category, and the bars are typically ordered by their height, is called a **bar diagram / histogram.**

3.4. The two graphs that are used to depict frequency distributions are the frequency polygon and the **bar diagram / histogram.**

3.5. In drawing histograms, the lower scores are recorded on the **left / right** side of the scores axis (the horizontal axis).

3.6. Frequency polygons are likely to look smoother as the number of scores **increases / decreases.**

3.7. The type of graph that can best show how different subgroups in a distribution relate to each other and how the proportions of the different subgroups add up to 100% is the **bar diagram / pie graph.**

3.8. The median, skewness, and spread of a distribution are best depicted using a **box plot / line graph.**

3.9. The distributions of scores from two groups that have taken the same test can more easily be compared to each other using a **histogram / frequency polygon.**

Choose the most appropriate graphs for the sets of data in the following questions and explain your choices:

3.10. Following is a list of the 4 most popular books chosen by 83 boys and 85 girls in the fourth-grade at Washington school (see Table 3.10). The list shows the *percentages* of girls and boys who read each of the 4 books.

Table 3.10.   Book Choices by Boys and Girls

Gender	Book A	Book B	Book C	Book D
Boys	81	69	55	65
Girls	63	65	80	58

a. What is the best graph to present these data and show gender differences in book selection? Following are three graphs for you to choose from; explain your choice. The choices are (a) a joint bars graph (Figure 3.10.1); (b) a line graph (Figure 3.10.2); and (c) two bar graphs (Figure 3.10.3).

b. Are there gender differences in book choices? Explain.

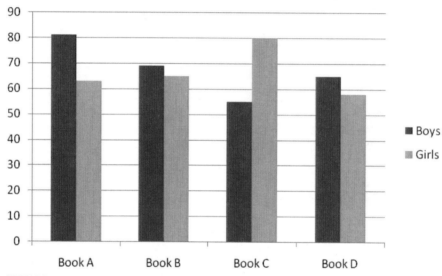

FIGURE 3.10.1
A joint bars graph

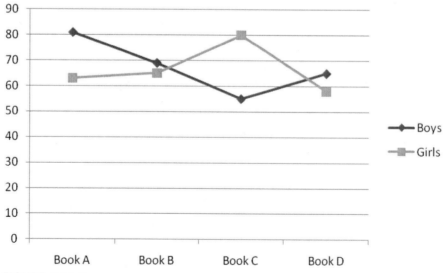

FIGURE 3.10.2
A line graph

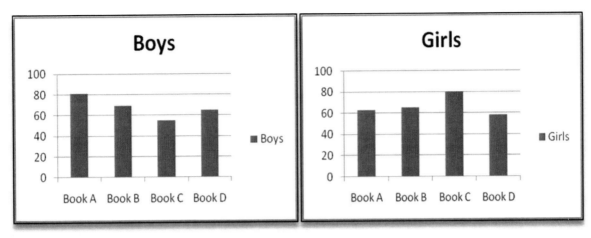

FIGURE 3.10.3
Bar graphs

3.11. Table 3.11 shows the mean test scores of three 8th-grade classes (8a, 8b, and 8c) over the years 2008 to 2011.

Table 3.11. Mean Test Scores of Three 8th-Grade Classes from 2008 to 2011

Class	Year 2008	Year 2009	Year 2010	Year 2011
8a	58	69	60	74
8b	70	55	75	78
8c	62	63	63	62

a. Choose the *best* graph to display these data and show changes in test scores over time from these two choices: (a) joint bars graph (Figure 3.11.1), and (b) line graph (Figure 3.11.2). Explain your choice.

b. Study the graph that you choose and explain the changes over time for the three 8th-grade classes.

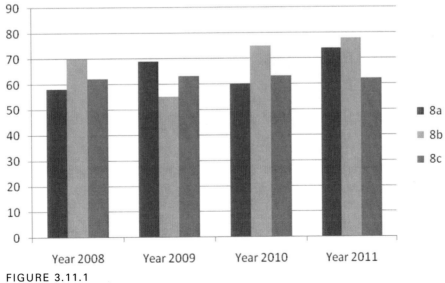

FIGURE 3.11.1
Joint bars graph

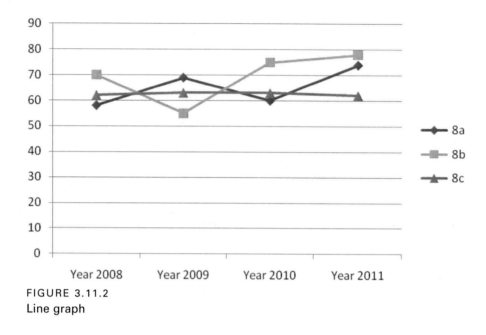

FIGURE 3.11.2
Line graph

3.12. Table 3.12 shows the distributions of race / ethnic groups in the district for the years 2000 and 2010, reported in *percentages*. The number of students in the district remained approximately the same over these 10 years.

Table 3.12.   Distribution of Racial / Ethnic Groups in a School District in 2000 and 2010

Group	2000	2010
Asians	10%	12%
African Americans	25%	31%
Hispanics	10%	15%
White	42%	30%
Others	13%	12%
TOTAL	100%	100%

a. Which graph would be the most appropriate to compare the racial / ethnic distributions in 2000 and 2010? Choose from the following three choices: (a) line graph (Figure 3.12.1), (b) two bar graphs (Figure 3.12.2), and (c) two pie graphs (Figure 3.12.3). Explain your choice.

b. Has there been a change in the racial / ethnic distribution from 2000 to 2010? Explain.

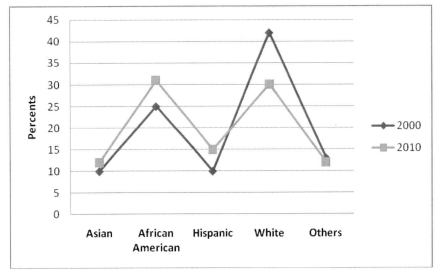

FIGURE 3.12.1
A line graph

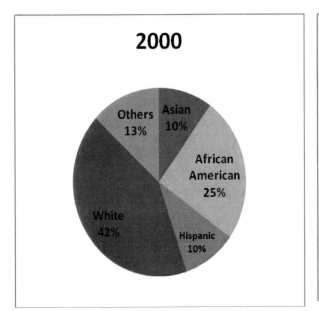
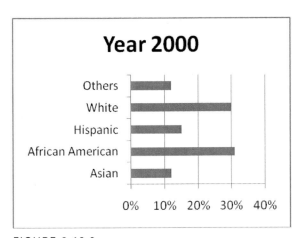

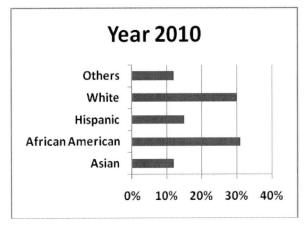
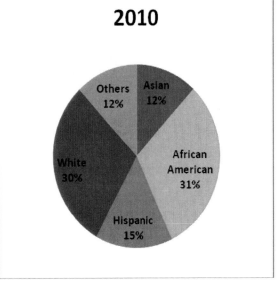

FIGURE 3.12.2
Two bar graphs

FIGURE 3.12.3
Two pie graphs

CHAPTER 3 ANSWERS

(3.1)   high. (Explanation: Where there is a limited range of scores [usually less than 20], there is no need to group them into class intervals.)

(3.2)   cumulative frequencies. (Explanation: Cumulative frequencies are designed to show the number of scores at, below, or above a given score. Class intervals show only the number of those who scored at each interval.)

(3.3)   bar diagram. (Explanation: A bar diagram is used for discrete and independent categories. A histogram is used for data that are on a continuum, in numerical order, such as calendar years or test scores.)

(3.4)   histogram. (Explanation: A histogram can also be used for depicting frequency distributions, while a bar diagram is used for showing several independent categories.)

(3.5)   left. (Explanation: The intersection of the two axes—the vertical and the horizontal—represents the lowest scores on these axes.)

(3.6)   increases. (Explanation: With more scores, the shape of the frequency polygon will look more like a normal distribution.)

(3.7)   pie graph. (Explanation: In pie graphs, the different wedges add up to 100%, unlike a bar diagram which shows independent categories, each with its own percentages or points.)

(3.8)   box plot. (Explanation: A box plot is the best graph to show the distribution's median, skewness, and spread. A line graph can show trends and changes over time.)

(3.9)   frequency polygon. (Explanation: Because a histogram is comprised of a series of bars, it is harder to show two or more groups using a histogram, whereas it is easier to show more than one group using a frequency polygon.)

(3.10)   a. The best graph to display the data is the first one, 3.10.1—a joint bars graph. The joint bar graph shows side-by-side the choices of the boys and girls and allows for easy comparison. The second choice, line graph, implies continuity whereas the books are independent and discrete units and are not on a continuum. The third choice, the two bar graphs, do not allow for easy comparison of the choices made by boys and girls, compared with the joint bars graph.

         b. Yes, there are gender differences. Book A was chosen more by boys than by girls; Book C was chosen more by girls than by boys. There were only small gender differences in the choices of Books B and D.

(3.11)   a. The best graph to display the data in Table 3.11 is the line graph (choice b). It can best show trends over time for the three groups. The first choice, the joint bars graph, makes it difficult to compare the groups to each other and see trends over time.

         b. Group 8a went up, down, and up again. Group 8b, which started the highest, also finished the highest, slightly higher than group 8a. Group 8b had the biggest annual changes between 2008 and 2010. Groups 8a and 8b were close to each other in 2010. The line graph shows that the mean scores of group 8c remained pretty constant over the 4-year period and ended up with the lowest mean score in 2011.

(3.12)   a. The best graph would be Figure 3.12.3 (choice c)—the two pie graphs. They can best show the demographic data side-by-side and how they changed from 2000 and 2010. The line graph in Figure 3.12.1 (choice a) implies continuity whereas the groups depicted are independent and are not in a numerical order on a continuum. This line graph does not show the relationship of the different groups to each other, and how they add up to 100% for each of the two years depicted. The bar graphs in Figure 3.12.2 (choice b) are not an efficient way to depict the data; they do not indicate that the various groups depicted add up to 100%; and they imply that the bars are ordered in some way, when, in fact, the racial / ethnic groups are not ordered nor are they on a continuum.

b. The number of white students decreased from 2000 to 2010. The numbers of the other racial / ethnic groups went up slightly over the same 10 years.

CHAPTER 3 SUPPLEMENTAL MICROSOFT™ EXCEL EXERCISES

Note: Access the datasets and exercises online at www.evalsolutions.net/portal/workbook.

Tech Tips

On the "Insert" menu, there are two bar graph options.

To create a bar graph with vertical bars for both pretest and posttest, highlight the data in the spreadsheet and click on the graph icon on the toolbar. Select "column" as the graph type on the Insert menu (data are in rows)

Use the Data Analysis option under the Tools menu to calculate descriptive statistics, including measures of central tendency and variability. Check the "Summary Statistics" option in the descriptive statistics dialog box.

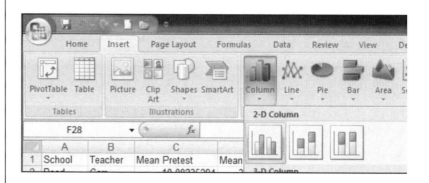

S3.1. Open the "DRA.xls" datafile.

S3.2. Click on the "Summary" tab to see mean pretest and posttest scores for all teachers. Generate a bar graph displaying mean pretest and posttest scores for teachers at Reed Elementary. (Specify data in "Rows" to create Pretest and Posttest scores for the X axis.)

a) Do students score higher on the pretest or posttest?

b) How do the results compare across the classrooms?

S3.3. Generate a scatterplot displaying the relationship between Pretest and Posttest scores for all Reed elementary data.

    a) Describe how the scores are spread out on the graph. Are there any clusters of dots? What does this tell you about the relationship between students' scores on the pretest and posttest?

    b) Find the students who received a Pretest DRA score of 15. What were their Posttest scores?

    c) Describe the spread of the dots for Pretest scores below 20 versus Pretest scores above 20.

    d) Is there more variability for low Pretest scores or for high Pretest scores? What does this mean about student performance?

CHAPTER 3. ANSWERS FOR MICROSOFT™ EXCEL EXERCISES
(S3.2)

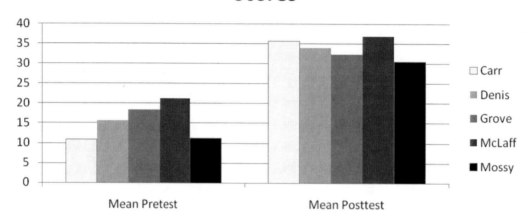

a) Students' scores are higher for the posttest.

b) The trend is similar across all teachers. All students' posttest scores are higher than their pretest scores. But Carr's classroom gained the most from pretest to posttest. Another way to depict the pre-to-post changes is to generate a pair of bar graphs for each teacher (pre- and posttest for each). Simply "right-click" the chart, choose "Select Data," and click the "Switch the Row / Column" option.

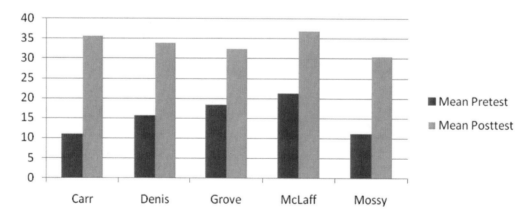

(S3.3)

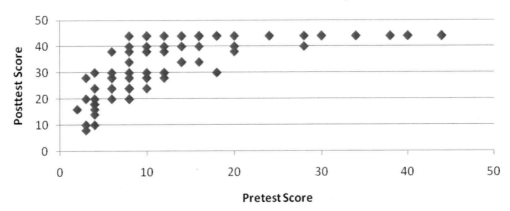

a) There are clusters of dots starting on the bottom left and continuing to about the middle of the graph (up to Pretest score = 20) with a single row of dots on the right half of the graph. The pattern shows that students with higher scores on the pretest tend to have higher scores on the posttest and vice versa.

b) Posttest scores = 34, 40, 44.

c) The Pretest scores below 20 are more spread out than the Pretest scores above 20. Regardless of their pretest scores, all students who scored over 20 on the pretest had the same posttest score (of 45).

d) For low Pretest scores—there is a larger range of scores on the Posttest for students scoring low on the Pretest. This indicates that there are more differences in the Posttest scores of students who scored below 20 on the Pretest; their Posttest scores are less consistent as a group. There may be other variables needed to explain their Posttest scores other than their Pretest scores.

4

Measure of Central Tendency

Fill in the blanks:

4.1.   The middle point of the distribution that divides it into the top 50% and the bottom 50% is called the _____.

4.2.   The descriptive statistic used the most in inferential statistics as a measure of central tendency is the _____.

4.3.   The measure of central tendency used with nominal scale data is the _____.

4.4.   To find the mean of a sample, the sum of the scores (ΣX) is divided by _____.

4.5.   Distributions that have more than 2 modes are called _____ distributions.

Circle the correct answer:

Using the following graphs, answer questions 4.6–4.9. The line inside each graph shows the mean of that distribution:

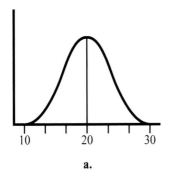
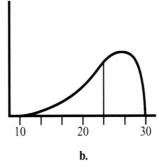
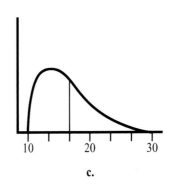

a.   b.   c.

a. Normal distribution   b. Negatively Skewed   c. Positively skewed

4.6.   In a *positively* skewed distribution, the majority of the scores cluster **above / below** the mean.

4.7.   The mode and the mean have the same values in distributions that are **normal / negatively skewed**.

4.8.   The mean is higher than the mode in **negatively / positively** skewed distributions.

4.9.   The median is higher than the mean in **negatively / positively** skewed distributions.

4.10. In statistics, $\bar{X}$ represents the mean of the **population / sample** and μ represents the mean of the **population/ sample**.

4.11. In statistics, we often use $\bar{X}/\mu$ to estimate $\bar{X}/\mu$.

Answer the following questions:

4.12. Which measure of central tendency would be the most appropriate for summarizing the following test scores? Explain your choice.

13, 14, 10, 38, 11, 12, 16, 15

4.13. A distribution of 10 scores has a mean of 6. Following are 9 scores of this distribution. Which score is missing (remember that the mean should be 6)?

4, 8, 10, 5, 9, 3, 6, 7, 3

4.14. When the sum of a group of scores is 280 and the mean of the scores is 7, how many scores are in the distribution?

4.15. Find the mode, median, and mean of the distribution depicted in the following histogram:

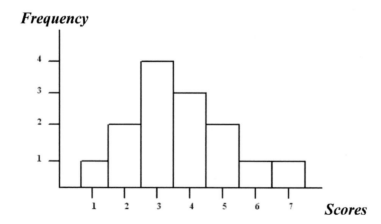

The mode is: _____
The median is: _____
The mean is: _____

CHAPTER 4 ANSWERS

(4.1)   median.

(4.2)   mean.

(4.3)   mode.

(4.4)   the number of the scores.

(4.5)   multimodal.

(4.6)   below. (Explanation: Because the mean is pulled toward the high extreme scores, the mean is higher than the majority of the scores.)

(4.7)   normal. (Explanation: In normal distributions, the mode, median, and mean have the same value; this is not the case with negatively or positively skewed distributions.)

(4.8)   positively. (Explanation: In positively skewed distributions, the mean is pulled toward the tail [which is on the right side in this case] whereas the mode is the peak of the distribution. The mean is farther along the scores axis and therefore it is a higher score.)

(4.9)   negatively. (Explanation: In a negatively skewed distribution, the mean is pulled toward the tail [which is on the left side in this case]. The median is a point that divides the distribution into two halves and this would be on the right side of the mean; therefore, it would be a higher score.)

(4.10) sample; population. (Explanation: $\bar{X}$ represents the sample mean; μ represents the population mean, because Greek letters are used for population values.)

(4.11) $\bar{X}$; μ. (Explanation: Samples are usually selected in order to study the population; therefore, the sample mean $\bar{X}$, is used to estimate the population mean μ.)

(4.12) median. (Explanation: There is no mode and the mean of 16.13 is higher than 7 out of 8 scores in the distribution; therefore, the median should be used.)

(4.13) 5. (Explanation: The sum of the scores should be 60 if there are 10 scores and the mean is 6. Adding up the 9 scores listed in the distribution gives us 55; therefore, the missing 10th score is 5.)

(4.14) 40.(Explanation: To find the number of scores, divide the sum of 280 by the mean of the scores, which is 7);

(4.15) mode = 3, median = 3.5, mean = 3.71. (Explanation: Following is a list of the scores depicted in the histogram and their frequency. This list would be helpful in computing the mode, median, and mean of the distribution.

Score	Frequency	Score × Frequency
1	1	1
2	2	4
3	4	12
4	3	12
5	2	10
6	1	6
7	1	7
Total	14	52

As can be seen, the mode is the score of 3 [it repeats 4 times] and the median is 3.5 [7 scores are above it and 7 scores are below it]. There are 14 scores in the distribution and the sum of the scores is 52 [the total of the third column], giving us a mean of 3.71.)

CHAPTER 4 SUPPLEMENTAL MICROSOFT™ EXCEL EXERCISES

Tech Tips

To create a line graph with lines for both pretest and posttest, highlight the data in the spreadsheet and click on the graph icon on the toolbar. Select the line type with markers displayed at each data point.

Use the Data Analysis option under the Tools menu to calculate descriptive statistics, including measures of central tendency and variability.

Check the "Summary Statistics" option in the descriptive statistics dialog box.

S4.1. Open the "DRA.xls" datafile.

S4.2. Compute median scores for all Pretest and Posttest DRA scores for Moore Elementary. Repeat for Reed Elementary. Create a 2 × 2 table in Excel with the school names in the rows and "Pretest Median" and "Posttest Median" for the columns. Complete the table using data from your descriptive analyses.

S4.3. Generate a line graph displaying the median pretest and posttest scores for Moore and Reed.

a) Compare the schools at the pretest.

b) Compare the schools at the posttest.

c) Describe the change for both schools from pretest to posttest.

d) Calculate the mean, median, and mode for all posttest scores at Moore Elementary. Which measure is the best estimate for these DRA data (considering whether DRA scores are nominal, ordinal, interval, or ratio)? How do outliers in the data affect the different measures?

CHAPTER 4 ANSWERS FOR MICROSOFT™ EXCEL EXERCISES

(S4.2) Median Pretest/Posttest Scores for Moore and Reed

	Pretest Median	Posttest Median
Moore	16	38
Reed	12	38

(S4.3)

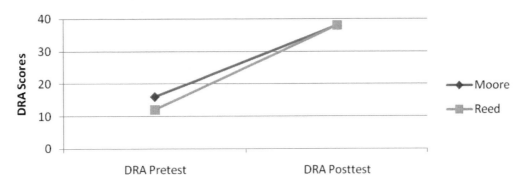

Pretest and Posttest Median DRA Scores

for Moore and Reed School

a) The schools are very similar at pretest, with Moore students scoring slightly higher.
b) The schools are the same at the posttest.
c) There is a dramatic increase in the median for the scores from the pretest to the posttest for both schools.
d) Posttest Mean = 33.87, median = 38, mode = 40. The median and mode are slightly higher than the mean. Because DRA scores are ranks (ordinal data), the median score is the best estimate of central tendency. Outliers have the greatest impact on the mean.

5

Measures of Variability

Circle the correct answer between the choices in bold:

5.1. The distance between the highest and the lowest scores is called the **range / variance**.

5.2. The SD is equal to the square root of the **mean / variance**.

5.3. A test with 30 items is likely to have a **higher / lower** standard deviation that a test with 90 items.

5.4. The mean of all the squared deviation scores of a given distribution is called the **variance / standard deviation**.

5.5. The SD of students in a gifted class taking a mathematics test is likely to be **higher / lower** than the SD of students in a diverse-ability multi-age class taking the same test.

5.6. The SD **is / is not** sensitive to extreme scores.

5.7. The variance of the *population* is represented by S^2 / σ^2.

5.8. In most cases, the variance is **larger / smaller** than the SD.

5.9. The measure of variability that takes into consideration and is affected by *every* score in the distribution is the **range / standard deviation**.

Answer / compute the following questions:

5.10. Three 4th-grade classes (4a, 4b, and 4c), each with 26 students, took the same language arts test. The SD of 4a was 7; the SD of 4b was 16; and the SD of 4c was 10. Which class was more *homogeneous* in regard to the scores on the language arts test?

5.11. Study the following three groups, each with 5 scores:

Group A: 8, 9, 6, 12, 5
Group B: 7, 10, 11, 8, 4
Group C: 7, 9, 8, 9, 7

a. What are the similarities and differences between the three groups in terms of their means and ranges?
b. Which group would you predict to have the smallest standard deviation and why?

5.12. A Total Reading test with 45 items is comprised of two subsections: (a) *Reading Comprehension* with 20 items, and (b) *Vocabulary* with 25 items. Means and standard deviations were calculated for the full-length test as well as for the two subsections. Estimate which of the following standard deviations was obtained for the *Total* Reading test and which standard deviation was obtained for the *Vocabulary* subtest.

a. SD = 5.7
b. SD = 8.3

5.13. Eight judges were selected to judge the statewide gymnastic competition. As part of their training, all judges observed a videotape of one gymnast in competition, and were asked to assign the gymnast a rating on a scale of 1–10. After 1 week of training and workshops, the eight judges were asked again to watch the same videotape, and rate the gymnast's performance, using the same scale of 1–10.

Review the scores of the eight judges in Table 5.13 and the box plot in Figure 5.13. Is there a difference between the pretraining and posttraining rating scores? What effect, if any, did the training have on the judges? Explain.

Table 5.13. Pretraining and Posttraining Scores of Eight Judges

Judge	Pretraining	Posttraining
A	9.5	9.1
B	7.8	8.9
C	9.9	9.1
D	8.6	8.8
E	8.2	8.8
F	9.6	9.0
G	8.6	8.9
H	9.1	9.0
Mean	**8.91**	**8.95**
SD	**0.73**	**0.12**

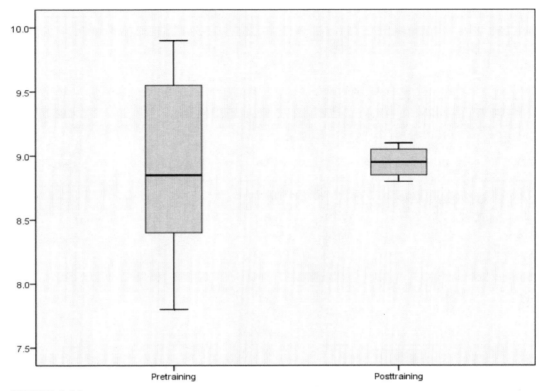

FIGURE 5.13
A box plot showing the scores assigned to the gymnast before and after training by the eight judges

5.14. Following is a graph showing two distributions of scores of two seventh-grade classes who had taken the same test. The means and standard deviations of the two groups are also given. *Estimate* which of the two means and which of the two SDs belong to each group of students.

Mean = 53   SD = 7
Mean = 69   SD = 15

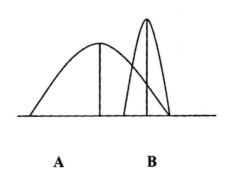

a. Group A: The mean is _____ and the SD is _____.
b. Group B: The mean is _____ and the SD is _____.

CHAPTER 5 ANSWERS

(5.1)   range. (Explanation: The range is an index of the difference between the highest and lowest scores in the distribution while the variance is the mean squared deviations around the mean.)

(5.2)   variance. (Explanation: The variance is directly related to the SD. To find the variance, we square the SD; to find the SD, we find the square root of the variance.)

(5.3)   lower. (Explanation: Because the standard deviation is the mean of the deviations around the mean, distributions with more items are likely to have more scores that are farther away from the mean, both above or below the mean.)

(5.4)   variance. (Explanation: The variance is an index of the squared deviations of scores around their mean.)

(5.5)   lower. (Explanation: There are likely to be fewer differences and less variability in the scores of students in a gifted class compared with a diverse-ability multi-age class.)

(5.6)   is. (Explanation: SD is an index of the mean deviation of the scores around their mean. Extreme scores would cause that mean deviation to be higher, compared with distributions where the scores tend to cluster close to the mean.)

(5.7) σ^2. (Explanation: Greek letters are used to represent population values.)

(5.8)   larger. (Explanation: The SD is the square root of the variance.)

(5.9)   standard deviation. (Explanation: The range is determined by the highest and lowest scores in the distribution only and it is not affected by scores between these upper and lower boundaries.)

(5.10) 4a. (Explanation: The SD of 4a is the lowest.)

(5.11) a. The means of the three groups are 8; the ranges of Groups A and B are the same (range=7); the range of Group C is the smallest (range=3).

b. We would expect the standard deviation of Group C to be the smallest since the scores in that group are closer to each other (the smallest range) in this group, compared with Groups A and B.

(5.12) The SD of the Total Reading test is 8.3 and the SD of the Vocabulary test is 5.7. (Explanation: The Total Reading test, with 45 items, is longer than the Vocabulary test, with 25 items; therefore, it is expected to have a higher SD.)

(5.13) The means of pretraining and posttraining scores are about the same, but the SD of the posttraining scores is much smaller. It seems that, as a result of the training, the 8 judges are better informed and more consistent in the scores they assign (a lower SD on the posttraining scores). Figure 5.13 shows that the scores are closer to each other in the second box (that shows the posttraining scores) compared with the pretraining box. This can be seen by both a smaller box and shorter whiskers for the posttraining score.

(5.14) Group A: mean = 53, SD = 15; Group B: mean = 69, SD = 7. (Explanation: The mean of Group B is higher than the mean of Group A because it is further on the right of the score axis, and scores on the right side of this axis are higher than the left side. The SD of Group A is higher than the SD of Group B because there is a wider spread of scores in Group A.)

CHAPTER 5 SUPPLEMENTAL MICROSOFT™ EXCEL EXERCISES

S5.1. Open the "ITBS.xls" datafile.

```
Tech Tips

Use the Data Analysis option
under the Tools menu to
calculate descriptive statistics,
including measures of central
tendency and variability.

Check the "Summary Statistics"
option in the descriptive
statistics dialog box.
```

S5.2. Calculate the standard deviation, variance, and range for the five variables (Grade, Reading S.S., Language S.S., and Math S.S.).

S5.3. Review the analysis results to answer these questions.

   a) Compare the standard deviation for the three measures.

   b) Compare the variance for the three measures.

   c) Compare the range for the three measures.

S5.4. Review the analysis results to answer these questions.

   a) Which variable (reading, language, and math) shows the **highest variations** (or differences) in responses by the students? How can you tell?

   b) Which variable (reading, language, and math) shows the **most similar** responses by the students?

   c) What do these trends mean about students' achievement on these subtests?

S5.5. Evaluate the statistics you calculated for the above variables. Do any of them seem inappropriate? Explain.

CHAPTER 5 ANSWERS FOR MICROSOFT™ EXCEL EXERCISES

(S5.2)

GEND.		GRADE		READ (S.S.)		MATH (S.S.)		LANG (S.S.)	
Mean	1.56	Mean	0.98	Mean	153.82	Mean	150.12	Mean	150.84
Std. Err	0.03	Std. Err	0.05	Std. Err	1.43	Std. Err	0.98	Std. Err	1.08
Median	2	Median	1	Median	153	Median	150	Median	152
Mode	2	Mode	0	Mode	132	Mode	138	Mode	140
Stand. Dev.	0.5	Stand. Dev.	0.82	Stand. Dev.	24.99	Stand. Dev.	17.08	Stand. Dev.	18.79
Sample Var.	0.25	Sample Var.	0.68	Sample Var.	624.26	Sample Var.	291.87	Sample Var.	353.12
Kurt	−1.9	Kurt	−1.53	Kurt	1.85	Kurt	−0.52	Kurt	−0.61
Skew	−0.3	Skew	0.04	Skew	0.72	Skew	0.33	Skew	0.21
Range	1	Range	2	Range	165	Range	86	Range	99
Min	1	Min	0	Min	100	Min	110	Min	112
Max	2	Max	2	Max	265	Max	196	Max	211
Sum	480	Sum	301	Sum	46915	Sum	46089	Sum	45856
Count	307	Count	307	Count	305	Count	307	Count	304

*Note: Decimals rounded

(S5.3)

a) The standard deviations of math (SD = 17.08) and language (SD = 18.79) scores are similar. The standard deviation is slightly larger for reading (SD = 24.99). The standard deviation is less than 1.00 for gender and grade.

b) The variances of math (σ^2 = 291.87) and language (σ^2 = 353.12) scores are similar. The variance is slightly larger for reading (σ^2 = 624.26). The variance is less than 1.00 for gender and grade (σ^2 = 0.25; notice the variance is the square of the standard deviation).

c) The ranges of math and language scores are very similar. The range is larger for reading. The ranges for gender and grade are about the same. The values for the ranges are smaller than the variance but larger than the standard deviation for reading, math, and language scores.

(S5.4)

a) The reading scores show the most variation or differences in students. All three measures of student differences (standard deviation, variance, and range) are largest for reading.

b) The math scores show the similarity between students. All three measures of student differences (standard deviation, variance, and range) are smallest for math.

c) Students are more similar in their math achievement than they are in their reading achievement. The achievement differences in math are somewhat smaller than the achievement differences in reading for these students.

(S5.5)

Gender is a nominal variable. The scores are meaningless because the values hold no numerical information.

6

The Normal Curve and Standard Scores

Circle the best answer:

6.1. In a normal distribution _____

  a. the mean and median have the same value.
  b. the mean and SD have the same value.
  c. the median and SD have the same value.
  d. the SD is always higher than the mean.

6.2. In a normal curve, the percentage of scores between a z score of 0 and a z score of +1 _____

  a. is the same as the percentage of scores between z scores of 1 and 2.
  b. is the same as the percentage between z scores of 0 and −1.
  c. changes as the mean changes.
  d. cannot be estimated without further information.

6.3. A z score of −1 converts to a T score of _____

  a. −1.
  b. 40.
  c. 60.
  d. 100.

6.4. A *negatively* skewed distribution indicates that the scores are _____

  a. distributed evenly above and below the mean.
  b. mostly negative.
  c. mostly low and below the mean.
  d. mostly high and above the mean.

6.5. When a student has a *z* score of 0 it means that the student _____

a. scored above most classmates.
b. scored below most classmates.
c. scored at the mean.
d. failed the test.

6.6. In a *positively* skewed distribution, which of the following two scores is likely to be the mean and which the median?

a. 23.50
b. 29.00

6.7. In a *negatively* skewed distribution, which of the following two scores is likely to be the mean and which the median?

a. 52.00
b. 60.00

6.8. When a student has a percentile rank of 45 it means that the student _____

a. answered correctly 45% of the test questions.
b. performed better than 45% of the examinees.
c. answered correctly 45 questions on the test.

6.9. A *T* score of 70 is equivalent to a percentile rank of _____

a. 50.
b. 70.
c. 84.
d. 98.

Circle the correct answer between the choices in bold:

6.10. If a student receives a *z* score of –1, it means that the student scored **above / below** the mean.

6.11. As the number of scores *decreases*, the shape of the distribution is likely to become **smoother / less smooth**.

6.12. The percentage of scores that lies between ±1SD is **68 / 95**.

6.13. A person with a *z* score of +1 scored better than **48% / 84%** of the examinees.

6.14. A *negative z* score converts to a *T* score that is **above / below** 50.

Answer/compute the following questions:

6.15. Following are 3 sets of measures of central tendency (mode, median, and mean). Estimate which set represents a normal distribution, a negatively skewed distribution, and a positively skewed distribution. Explain your answer.

	Mode	Median	Mean
Set A	25	22	16
Set B	25	27	31
Set C	25	25	25

Set A: _____ distribution.

Set B: _____ distribution.

Set C: _____ distribution.

6.16. Following are test scores obtained by Linda on four tests (Test A, Test B, Test C, and Test D), as well as the means and standard deviations on the same four tests.

Test	Linda's Score	Mean	SD
Test A	54	50	8
Test B	30	27	3
Test C	69	66	6
Test D	61	62	5

Compare Linda's scores on the four tests and answer the following:

a. On which test did Linda do the best?

b. On which test did Linda perform the lowest?

c. On which two tests did Linda do equally well?

(Note: To answer these questions, you may want to start by converting Linda's scores on the four tests to *z* scores.)

Use the figure below to answer questions 6.17 and 6.18:

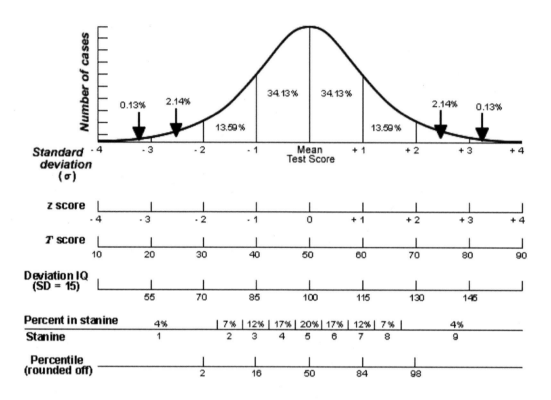

6.17. A social studies test has a mean of 18 and an SD of 5. Assuming that the scores are distributed normally and using the normal curve picture above, answer the following questions:

a. Maxine had a score of 23 on the test. What is her percentile rank?

b. We can estimate that 68% of the examinees that took the test scored between the score of _____ and the score of _____.

c. The top 2% of the students scored above the score of _____.

6.18. A high school geometry test has a mean of 31 and an SD of 6. Assuming that the scores are distributed normally and using the normal curve picture above, answer the following questions:

a. Joe had a score of 25 on the test. What is his percentile rank?

b. We can estimate that approximately 34% of the examinees that took the test scored between the score of 37 and the score of _____.

c. Approximately _____% of the examinees scored between the mean and the score of 43.

CHAPTER 6 ANSWERS

(**6.1**) a.

(**6.2**) b.

(**6.3**) b.

(**6.4**) d.

(**6.5**) c.

(**6.6**) The mean is 29.00 and the median is 23.50. (Explanation: In a positively skewed distribution, the mean is higher than the median, because extreme high scores [i.e., outliers] pull the mean toward them.)

(**6.7**) The mean is 52.00 and the median is 60.00. (Explanation: In a negatively skewed distribution, the median is higher than the mean, because extreme low scores [i.e., outliers] pull the mean toward them.)

(**6.8**) b. (Explanation: A percentile score indicates the percent of examinees who scored below [or at and below] that percentile score; therefore, a percentile of 45 means that the student performed better than 45% of the test takers.)

(**6.9**) d. (Explanation: An inspection of the normal curve indicates that a T score of 70 corresponds to a z score of +2 and to a percentile rank of 98.)

(**6.10**) below.

(**6.11**) less smooth.

(**6.12**) 68%.

(**6.13**) 84%.

(**6.14**) below.

(**6.15**) Set A is a negatively skewed distribution. (Explanation: In Set A, the mean is lower than the median, and the median is lower than the mode, which is typical of negatively skewed distributions.) Set B is a positively skewed distribution; (Explanation: In Set B, the mean is higher than the median, and the median is higher than the mode, which is typical of positively skewed distributions.) Set C is a normal distribution. (Explanation: In Set C, the mode, median, and mean have the same value, which is typical of normal distributions.)

(**6.16**) a. Test B. (Explanation: Linda's z score is +1.00.)

b. Test D. (Explanation: Linda's z score is –0.20.)

c. Tests A and C. (Explanation: On both tests, Linda's z scores are +0.50.)

(**6.17**) a. 84. (Explanation: Maxine scored 1SD above the mean and did better than 84% of the examinees.)

b. 13 and 23. (Explanation: These scores are equal to ±1SD, which includes 68% of the scores.)

c. 28. (Explanation: The top 2% of the students are found in the area that is above 2SD. The point of 2SD corresponds to a score of 28.)

Note: Using the picture of the normal curve, you may want to mark the center with the mean of 18. Because the SD is 5, move up and down the tick marks on the horizontal axis of the normal curve using increments of 5 points in each direction. Therefore, 1SD would correspond to a score of 23 (18 + 5) and 2SD would correspond to a score of 28. On the other side that is below the mean, –1SD would correspond to a score of 13 (18 – 5) whereas –2SD would correspond to a score of 8.

(**6.18**) a. 16. (Explanation: Joe's score of 26 is exactly 1SD below the mean (31 – 6 = 25) and –1SD corresponds to a percentile rank of 16.)

b. 31. (Explanation: 34% of the scores lie between the mean of 31 and the score of 37, which is 1SD above the mean.)

c. 48%. (Explanation: The mean is 31 and the SD is 6; therefore, there are 2SD between the mean and the score of 43. This distance includes approximately 48% of the examinees.)

7

Interpreting Test Scores

Circle the correct answer between the choices in bold:

7.1. A national norming group that is used by test publishers is usually comprised of examinees from a _____

   a. stratified random sample.
   b. random sample.
   c. sample of convenience.
   d. systematic sample.

7.2. A percentile of 50 corresponds to a stanine of _____

   a. 2.
   b. 5.
   c. 6.
   d. 9.

7.3. Stanine 6 includes the same number of examinees as stanine _____

   a. 1.
   b. 3.
   c. 4.
   d. 8.

7.4. In a norm-referenced test, the highest number of examinees is expected to score in stanine _____

   a. 1.
   b. 3.
   c. 5.
   d. 7.

Circle the correct answer between the choices in bold:

7.5. Items that are written specifically to *maximize* the differences among examinees are found usually in **criterion-referenced / norm-referenced** tests.

7.6. Overall, items in a criterion-referenced test are **easier / more difficult** than those in a norm-referenced test.

7.7. The percentile rank of a student who scored 1SD below the mean on a norm-referenced achievement test is **16 / 34**.

7.8. Easy items on a norm-referenced test are usually placed at the **end / beginning** of the test.

7.9. The *local* norms of students in a school district known for its high academic achievement scores are expected to be **higher / lower** than the *national* percentiles obtained by these students on the same test.

7.10. Manuals of commercial norm-referenced tests should include information about the demographic characteristics of the **sample / population** that was used to generate the test norms.

Fill in the blanks:

7.11. Prospective school psychologists are notified that they have to score at least 1SD above the mean in order to pass the state certification examination. The certification examination has mean of 50 and an SD of 12. In order to pass the examination, applicants should obtain a score of *at least* _____.

7.12. Students in a K–5 school district take a group IQ test. The teachers in that school district are told that they should refer to special services that are provided by the district all of their students who score 1SD below the mean, or lower, on the IQ test. The test has a mean of 100 and an SD of 15. Knowing this information, we can conclude that the IQ scores of students that are referred to the district's special services are not higher than _____.

7.13. A student who scored 500 on a norm-referenced test with a mean of 500 and an SD of 100, performed better than _____% of the students in the norming group that was used to generate the test norms.

7.14. In a school where students are tested at the same time each year, an average-level student who obtained a GE of 6.2 while in *sixth* grade is expected to get a GE of _____ when tested in the *seventh* grade.

CHAPTER 7 ANSWERS

(7.1) a.

(7.2) b.

(7.3) c.

(7.4) c.

(7.5) norm-referenced. (Explanation: Norm-referenced test is designed to spread the scores and create a bell shape distribution.)

(7.6) easier. (Explanation: Unlike norm-referenced tests, items on criterion-referenced tests are designed to be answered correctly by the majority of the students taking the test.)

(7.7) 16. (Explanation: Looking at the normal curve graph, we can see that students who score 1SD below the mean perform better than 16% of the examinees because they score about 34% below the mean.)

(7.8) beginning. (Explanation: Placing easier items near the beginning of the test is done to encourage and motivate the students taking the test.)

(7.9) lower. (Explanation: Local percentiles compare students to other high-ability students in the district, while the national percentiles compare students to the national norming sample that includes students with lower ability levels.)

(7.10) sample. (Explanation: Information about the demographic characteristics of the norming sample that was used by the publisher to generate the test norms helps test users determine whether that sample is similar to those taking the test.)

(7.11) 62. (Explanation: In a test with a mean of 50 and an SD of 12, a score of 62 is 1SD above the mean [50 + 12 = 62].)

(7.12) 85. (Explanation: An IQ score of 85 is 1SD below the mean; therefore, in order to be referred to these particular special services, students in the district cannot have IQ scores that are higher than 85.)

(7.13) 50. (Explanation: The score of 500 is exactly at the mean; therefore, the student performed better than 50% of those in the norming group.)

(7.14) 7.2. (Explanation: Average-level students are expected to move up 1GE each year.)

8

Correlations

Fill in the blanks:

8.1. The magnitude of the correlation is indicated by the correlation _____, which can range from −1.00 to +1.00.

8.2. The most common and efficient way to present the correlations of several variables with each other is by using a(n) _____ table.

8.3. The correlation between two variables can be shown *graphically* by a _____.

8.4. The null hypothesis predicts that the correlation coefficient is equal to _____.

8.5. The Spearman rank order correlation is used when the variables to be correlated are measured on a(n) _____ scale.

Circle the correct answer between the choices in bold:

8.6. The hypothesis that states that $r \neq 0$ is an example of a(n) **alternative / null** hypothesis.

8.7. When an *increase* in one variable is associated with a *decrease* in the other variable, the correlation between these two variables is **positive / negative**.

8.8. In order to use the Pearson product-moment correlation, the variables to be correlated should be measured on an **ordinal / interval** scale.

8.9. When the points on a scattergram go from the bottom left to the top right they represent a **positive / negative** correlation.

8.10. The true correlation between two variables may be *underestimated* when the variance of one of the variables is **very high / very low**.

8.11. When the null hypothesis is rejected at $p < .001$, it means that the likelihood that the correlation coefficient is equal to 0 ($r = 0$) is **very small / very high**.

8.12. The null hypothesis is rejected when the *obtained* correlation coefficient is **higher / lower** than the *critical* value.

Answer/compute the following questions:

8.13. Which correlation coefficient (*a* or *b*) shows a stronger relationship between the two variables being cor-related?

   a. $X_1 \& Y_1$: $r = .85$

   b. $X_2 \& Y_2$: $r = -.94$

8.14. Following are two scattergrams (in Figure A and in Figure B). Four different correlation coefficients are listed under each scattergram. Choose the coefficient that best matches each scattergram.

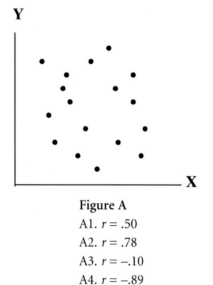

Figure A
A1. $r = .50$
A2. $r = .78$
A3. $r = -.10$
A4. $r = -.89$

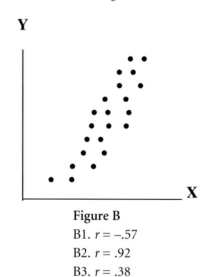

Figure B
B1. $r = -.57$
B2. $r = .92$
B3. $r = .38$
B4. $r = -.91$

8.15. What do these two scattergrams have in common?

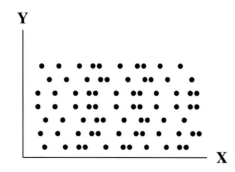

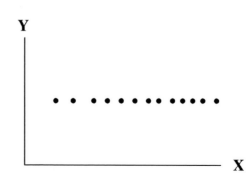

8.16. *Estimate* (do not *calculate!*) the correlation between Test X and Test Y scores that were obtained by 5 students. Indicate whether the correlation is positive or negative, and whether it is high or low. Explain your answer.

Student #	X	Y
1	21	83
2	15	70
3	17	68
4	25	90
5	19	74

8.17. *Estimate* (do not *calculate!*) which of the two sets of scores (A&B or X&Y) has a higher correlation. Explain your answer.

Set 1			Set 2		
Student #	A	B	Student #	X	Y
1	41	50	1	66	47
2	41	47	2	53	36
3	38	43	3	50	45
4	30	39	4	48	38
5	28	37	5	45	39

8.18. Match the correlation coefficient and the diagram illustrating this correlation.

a. $r = .91$

b. $r = .28$

c. $r = .15$

8.19. Study the following intercorrelation table. Two tests measure *language arts* and two tests measure *mathematics*. Knowing that Test 1 measures language arts, speculate which is the other language arts test (2, 3, or 4) and which two tests measure mathematics. (*A hint: the two language arts tests should correlate higher with each other than with the two mathematics tests, and the two mathematics tests should correlate higher with each other than with the two language arts tests.*)

	2	3	4
1	.35	.89	.23
2		.39	.92
3			.34

8.20. Following are results from a study correlating science and mathematics scores from a group of 16 boys, a group of 15 girls, and the two groups combined.

Table 8.20.   Correlations between Science and Mathematics by Gender

Group	Correlation (r)/ Group Size (n)/ Significance (p value)
Boys	r = .59
	n = 16
	p = .02
Girls	r = .52
	n = 15
	p = .05
Combined	r = .53
	n = 31
	p = .01

a. Which correlation coefficient is the highest?

b. Which correlation coefficient has the highest statistical significance?

c. How can a correlation of $r = .53$ (from the combined group) be more statistically significant (more significant p value) than a correlation of $r = .59$ (from the group of boys)?

CHAPTER 8 ANSWERS

(8.1)   coefficient.

(8.2)   intercorrelation.

(8.3)   scattergram.

(8.4)   zero.

(8.5)   ordinal.

(8.6)   alternative.

(8.7)   negative.

(8.8)   interval.

(8.9)   positive.

(8.10) very low.

(8.11) very small.

(8.12) higher.

(8.13) b. (Explanation: Even though the correlation coefficient of −.94 is negative, it represents a stronger relationship between the variable than the correlation coefficient of .84.)

(8.14) Figure A matches the correlation of $r = −.10$ in A3. (Explanation: The scattergram in Figure A shows a low negative correlation corresponding to $r = −.10$). Figure B matches the correlation of $r = .92$ in B2. (Explanation: The scattergram in Figure B shows a high positive correlation corresponding to $r = .92$.)

(8.15) Both scattergrams indicate very low or no correlation.

(8.16) The correlation is positive and very high. (Explanation: Start by rank-ordering the scores on X and then do the same for the scores on Y. The relative positions of the 5 students on the two tests are very similar, indicating a high positive correlation. Those who scored high on one test also scored high on the other test, and those who scored low on one test also scored low on the other test.)

(8.17) The correlation between A and B is higher than the correlation between X and Y. (Explanation: Start by rank ordering each set of scores and comparing the ranks. You can see that the ranks of the students on Test A are similar to their ranks on Test B [in Set 1], showing a high correlation. By comparison, the ranks of the students on Test X differ from their ranks on Test Y [in Set 2], showing a lower correlation.)

(8.18) a ($r = .91$). (Explanation: Start by squaring the three correlation coefficients to determine the *coefficients of determination*. This would reveal that the diagram most closely represents the correlation coefficient of $r = .91$. The diagram and this coefficient both show a high level of overlap [about 83%] and association between the two variables.)

(8.19) Tests 1&3 measure language arts, and Tests 2&4 measure mathematics. (Explanation: Tests 1 and 3 have a higher correlation with each other than with the other two tests and because Test 1 measures language arts, we can assume that Test 3 also measures language arts. Tests 2 and 4 have a higher correlation with each other than with the other two tests; therefore, we can assume that both tests measure mathematics.)

(8.20) a. The correlation of $r = .59$ (for the boys) is the highest. (Explanation: It is the highest r value.).

b. The correlation of $r = .53$ (for the two groups combined). (Explanation: The p value of this correlation is .01 and it is lower than the other two p values, which means that it has the highest level of significance.)

c. Because of differences in sample sizes. (Explanation: The correlation of $r = .53$ was computed for a group of 31, while the correlation of $r = .59$ was computed for a group of 16.)

CHAPTER 8 SUPPLEMENTAL MICROSOFT™ EXCEL EXERCISES

Tech Tips

Use the Data Analysis option under the Tools menu to calculate the correlation.

Generate the scatterplot for all data. For advanced users, use the "Series" tab to create separate clusters for kindergarten, first, and second graders.

S8.1. Open the "ITBS.xls" datafile.

S8.2. Investigate the relationship between students' reading scale scores and their math scale scores.

Write the hypothesized relationship:

a) Null Hypothesis:

b) Alternative Directional Hypothesis:

S8.3. Compute a correlation coefficient.

S8.4. Report the variable names and correlation.

S8.5. Is the correlation significant? (Assume the critical value $r = .095$ with a preset significance level=.05). Explain your answer.

S8.6. Describe the *magnitude* and *direction* of the correlation.

S8.7. What decision can you make about the null hypothesis?

S8.8. Create a scatterplot that shows the relationship between the math and reading scores. Are there any outliers?

CHAPTER 8 ANSWERS FOR MICROSOFT™ EXCEL EXERCISES

(S8.2)

a) Null Hypothesis: The correlation of reading and math scale scores = 0, or There is no significant correlation between reading and math scores.

b) Alternative Directional Hypothesis: The correlation of reading and math scale scores is > 0, or There is a significant positive correlation between reading and math scores.

(S8.4)

	Reading (S.S.)	Math (S.S.)
Reading (S.S.)	1	
Math (S.S.)	0.735804	1

(S8.5)   The correlation is significant for a preset significance level = .001.

(S8.6)   The magnitude is .735, a strong relationship. The direction is positive. As reading scores go up, math scores go up. As reading scores go down, math scores go down. Reading scores are associated with math scores; those who score high on one variable also tend to score high on the other variable.

(S8.7)   Reject the null hypothesis with a preset significance level =.05 (We only want to risk a 5% chance of committing a Type 1 error before we compute the statistic. Our actual significance level shows even a lower actual risk of a Type 1 error). The data support the alternative hypothesis. There is a less than 1/10% chance of a Type 1 error. That is, there is less than 1/10% chance that we are rejecting the null hypothesis when it really is true.

(S8.8)

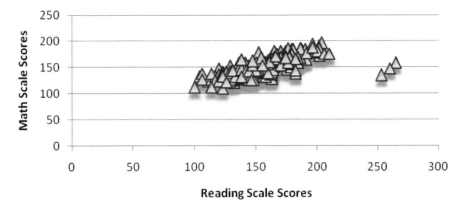

There appear to be 3 outliers for Reading scores over 250.

9

Prediction and Regression

Fill in the blanks:

9.1. In *simple* regression, there is/are _____ predictor(s).

9.2. The regression line is also called *a line* _____.

9.3. The slope of the regression line is represented by the letter _____.

9.4. When the regression equation is used to draw a line, the point where that line intersects the vertical line (the *Y*-axis) is represented by the letter _____ which indicates the *intercept*.

9.5. When the correlation between two variables is *perfect* and *positive*, and we use one of these variables to predict the other one, the *standard error of estimate* (S_E) is _____.

9.6. The difference between an actual *Y* score and its corresponding predicted *Y* score (*Y'*) is called the _____ score.

9.7. In *multiple* regression with *two* predictors, there is/are _____ intercept(s), represented in the equation by the letter *a*.

Circle the correct answer between the choices in bold:

9.8. In regression, the *predictor* is called the **independent / dependent** variable, and the *predicted* variable (or the *criterion* variable) is called the **independent / dependent**.

9.9. The *predicted* variable is represented by the letter *X / Y* and the *predictor* is represented by the letter *X / Y*.

9.10. In the regression equation, the letter *b* represents the **constant / coefficient** and the letter *a* represents the **constant / coefficient**.

9.11. The dependent variable can be predicted more accurately as the correlation between the independent and dependent variables **increases / decreases.**

9.12. As the correlation between the predictor and the criterion variable *increases*, the standard error of estimate (S_E) **increases / decreases.**

9.13. The predicted *Y* scores are expected to be **on / around** the regression line.

9.14. Scores on the criterion variable can be predicted more accurately when S_E is **larger / smaller.**

Answer/compute the following questions:

9.15. Study the following graph. If a student has a score of 25 on the Vocabulary Test (the predictor *X*), what is the student's predicted score on the Reading Test (the criterion *Y*)?

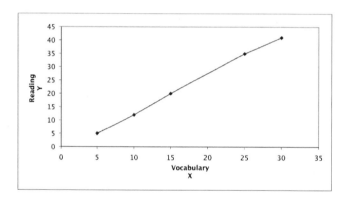

9.16. Compute S_E (the standard error of estimate) when the standard deviation of the *Y*-variable is 5 ($SD_Y = 5$) and the correlation is .00 ($r = .00$). Use the following equation to compute the S_E:

$$S_E = SD_Y\sqrt{1-r^2} =$$

What is the relationship between the S_E (the standard error of estimate) and the *SD* of the dependent variable *Y* ($SD_Y = 5$) when the correlation is zero ($r = .00$)? Explain.

9.17. A science teacher used the midterm and final scores of her last year's students to derive a prediction equation. This year's students, who are similar to last year's students, take the midterm exam, and their scores are used to predict their final grade. The teacher decided that to get a grade of A, students have to score from 90 to 100. To get a grade of B, the scores should be 80–89, and for a grade of C, the scores should be 70–79. Table 9.17 shows the midterm exam scores of 6 students, and the prediction equation.

   a. Calculate the students' predicted scores (*Y'* scores) on the end-of-year examination. (Note: Use the prediction equation to compute the students' *Y'* scores.)

   b. Calculate the students' predicted final grades (a grade of A, B, or C), based on their end-of-year examination scores.

Table 9.17. Midterm Scores of 6 Students

Student	Students' Midterm Scores X	Predicted Final Scores Y'	Predicted Grades
Jay	52		
Doreen	45		
Sam	54		
Michael	49		
Madison	42		
Rachel	55		

$$b = 1.5 \qquad a = 13.2$$
$$Y' = b(S) + \alpha$$

9.18. Figure A shows three predictors, X_1, X_2, and X_3, and their correlations with the criterion variable Y_1. Figure B shows three predictors, Z_1, Z_2, and Z_3, and their correlations with a criterion variable Y_2.

  a. Which predictor variables, those depicted in Figure A or those depicted in Figure B, correlate higher *with each other*?

  b. Which set of three predictors, those shown in Figure A (X_1, X_2, and X_3) or those shown in Figure B (Z_1, Z_2, and Z_3) is likely to predict the criterion variables (Y_1 or Y_2) more accurately?

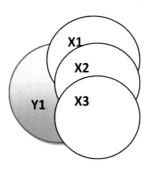

Figure A

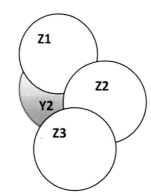

Figure B

CHAPTER 9 ANSWERS

(9.1) one.

(9.2) of best fit.

(9.3) *b.*

(9.4) a.

(9.5) zero.

(9.6) error.

(9.7) one.

(9.8) independent; dependent.

(9.9) *Y, X.*

(9.10) coefficient; constant.

(9.11) increases.

(9.12) decreases.

(9.13) on.

(9.14) smaller.

(9.15) 35. (Explanation: Draw a straight vertical line starting at the score of 25 on the *X*-axis [Vocabulary]. When that straight line hits the regression line, make a 90-degree angle and draw a horizontal line towards the *Y*-axis. That horizontal line will intersect the *Y*-axis at a Reading score of 35.)

(9.16) The S_E is 5, the same as the SD of the dependent variable (SD_Y). (Explanation: When the correlation is zero [$r = .00$], the standard error of estimate [S_E] is always equal to the SD of the *Y*-variable [the criterion variable].) The calculations are as follows:

$$S_E = SD_Y\sqrt{1-r^2} = 5\sqrt{1-.00^2} = 5\sqrt{1} = 5$$

(9.17) The predicted scores and letter grades are listed in the following table (Table 9.17)

Table 9.17. **Students' Scores on the Midterm Exam, Predicted Final Scores, and Letter Grades**

Student	Students' Midterm Scores X	Predicted Final Scores Y'	Predicted Grades
Jay	52	91.2	A
Doreen	45	80.7	B
Sam	54	94.2	A
Michael	49	86.7	B
Madison	42	76.2	C
Rachel	55	95.7	A

(Explanation: The prediction equation was used first to compute the students' *Y'* scores. Using the information provided in the question [$b = 1.5$; $a = 13.2$], we first create the prediction equation below. The prediction equation used for prediction is:

$$Y' = b(X) + a = 1.5(X) + 13.2$$

To compute each student's *Y'* score, the student's *X* score is entered into the equation. The predicted scores [*Y'* scores] are then converted into letter grades.)

(9.18) a. The three variables depicted in Figure A correlate higher with each other than the three variables depicted in Figure B. (Explanation: The variables in Figure A depict higher correlations between the predictors X_1, X_2, and X_3, because they overlap more than those in Figure B.)

b. The predictors shown in Figure B (Z_1, Z_2, and Z_3) are likely to predict the criterion variable Y_2 more accurately than the predictors shown in Figure A. (Explanation: The variables depicted in Figure B overlap less with each other than those in Figure A while also correlating with Y_2 and thus account for more of the variability in the criterion variable.)

CHAPTER 9 SUPPLEMENTAL MICROSOFT™ EXCEL EXERCISES

<table>
<tr><td>

Tech Tip

To compute a REGRESSION, select "Regression" from the Data-Analysis dialog box under "Tools" menu.

Highlight the columns of your independent (predictor) variables for "X" and dependent (outcome) variables for "Y" in the dialog box. Be sure to specify a 95% or more confidence interval.

</td></tr>
</table>

S9.1.   Open your "ITBS_REGRESSION.xls" datafile.

S9.2.   Investigate whether kindergarten and first grade reading scores are good predictors of second grade reading scores.

Compute a regression using kindergarten (X_1) and first grade scores (X_2) to predict second grade scores (Y).

Interpreting your REGRESSION results:

S9.3.   Complete the table based on results from your Microsoft® Excel analyses.

SUMMARY OUTPUT

Regression Statistics			
Multiple R			
R Square			
Adjusted R Square			
Standard Error			
Observations			
	Coefficients	Standard Error	P-value
Intercept			
Kindergarten READING (S.S.)			
First Grade READING (S.S.)			

S9.4. Identify the *predictor* and *dependent* variables in your analyses.

S9.5. Identify the R and *p* values.

S9.6. a) Identify R^2.

b) What does this indicate about the amount of variance accounted for by these independent variables?

c) Are the kindergarten and first grade scores good predictors of second grade scores?

S9.7. a) Based on your analyses, what is the value of knowing kindergarten and first grade scores in reading? How can educators use this information to predict student achievement?

b) How might keeping track of these scores over time be used as part of a school improvement plan?

CHAPTER 9 ANSWERS FOR MICROSOFT™ EXCEL EXERCISES

(S9.3)

SUMMARY OUTPUT

Regression Statistics	
Multiple R	0.94979
R Square	0.902101
Adjusted R Square	0.900018
Standard Error	6.541308
Observations	97

	Coefficients	Standard Error	P-value
Intercept	2.9854	14.74103	0.839944
Kindergarten READING (S.S.)	2.2627	0.32875	6.49E-10
First Grade READING (S.S.)	−0.7654	0.35416	0.033218

(S9.4) Kindergarten and first grade scores are the *predictors* and second grade score variable is the *dependent* variable.

(S9.5) R = .95, p = .00001. This is seen in the *Regression Statistics* table as "Multiple R" (number is rounded to the second decimal).

(S9.6) a) R^2 = .902. This is seen in the *Regression Statistics* table as "R Square" (number is rounded to the second decimal).

b) Kindergarten and first grade scores account for about 90% of the differences in second grade scores. The R Square (.90) is multiplied times 100 to obtain the percent of the differences.

c) Kindergarten and first grade scores are excellent predictors of second grade scores. Very little of the variance in second grade scores is left unaccounted for or unexplained.

(S9.7) a) Knowing kindergarten and first grade scores is valuable for identifying patterns in student achievement. It is likely that students' scores will be similar in second grade.

b) A school might use kindergarten and first grade achievement scores *in conjunction with* classroom-based indicators (like report cards and portfolios) to identify student learning needs. Second grade teachers can adapt instruction based on analyses of all data.

10

t Test

Fill in the blanks:

10.1. In a *t* test for a single sample, the sample's mean is compared to the population's _____.

10.2. When we use a paired-samples *t* test to compare the pretest and posttest scores for a group of 45 people, the degrees of freedom (*df*) are _____.

10.3. If we conduct a *t* test for independent samples, and $n_1 = 32$ and $n_2 = 35$, the degrees of freedom (*df*) are _____.

10.4. A researcher wants to study the effect of college education on people's earning by comparing the annual salaries of a randomly selected group of 100 college graduates to the annual salaries of 100 randomly selected group of people whose highest level of education is high school. To compare the mean annual salaries of the two groups, the researcher should use a *t* test for _____.

10.5. A technology coordinator and a science teacher in a middle school want to determine the effectiveness of a program that makes extensive use of educational technology in eighth-grade science classes. They compare the science scores of the eighth graders in the school on a state-administered test to the mean score of *all* eighth-grade students in the state on the same test. The appropriate statistical test the coordinator and the teacher should use for their analysis is the *t* test for _____.

10.6. As part of the process to develop two parallel forms of a questionnaire, a test constructor administers both forms to a group of students, and then uses a *t* test for _____ samples to compare the mean scores on the two forms.

Circle the correct answer between the choices in bold:

10.7. When a *t* test for paired samples is used to compare the pretest and the posttest means, the number of pretest scores is **the same as / different than** the number of posttest scores.

10.8.   When we want to compare whether girls' scores on the SAT are different from boys' scores, we should use a *t* test for **paired samples / independent samples.**

10.9.   In studies where the alternative (research) hypothesis is *directional*, the critical values for a **one-tailed test / two-tailed test** should be used to determine the level of significance (i.e., the *p* value).

10.10. When the alternative hypothesis is: $H_A: \mu_1 = \mu_2$, the critical values for **one-tailed test / two-tailed test** should be used to determine the level of statistical significance.

10.11. A difference of 4 points between two *homogeneous* groups is likely to be **more / less** statistically significant than the same difference (of 4 points) between two *heterogeneous* groups, when all four groups are taking the same test and have approximately the same number of students.

10.12. A difference of 3 points on a 100-item test taken by two groups is likely to be **more / less** statistically significant than a difference of 3 points on a 30-item test taken by the same two groups.

Answer/compute the following questions:

10.13. Study the following formula for a *t* test for independent samples. What measures (e.g., the mean of Group 1) are needed in order to calculate the *t* value? (Respond in words, not symbols).

$$t = \frac{\overline{X}_1 - \overline{X}_2}{\sqrt{\dfrac{(n_1 - 1)S_1^2 + (n_2 - 1)S_2^2}{n_1 + n_2 - 2}\left(\dfrac{1}{n_1} + \dfrac{1}{n_2}\right)}}$$

10.14. Identify each of the following as a *null* hypothesis, a *directional* hypothesis, or a *nondirectional* hypothesis.

        a. $\mu_1 \neq \mu_2$ is a _____ hypothesis
        b. $\mu_1 = \mu_2$ is a _____ hypothesis
        c. $\mu_1 > \mu_2$ is a _____ hypothesis
        d. $\mu_1 - \mu_2 = 0$ is a _____ hypothesis

10.15. In a study conducted to compare the test scores of experimental and control groups, a 50-item test is administered to both groups at the end of the study. The mean of the experimental group on the test is 1 point higher than the mean of the control group. The researchers conduct a *t* test for independent samples to compare the two means. The *obtained t* value is 1.89, and the *p*-value is .05. Can we conclude that the experimental treatment was *clearly effective* because the *t* value is *statistically significant*? Explain.

10.16. A school psychologist wants to compare the scores of a group of 35 students on two different IQ tests: one is a group IQ test and one is an individually administered IQ test. Both tests have a mean of 100 and an SD of 15. The psychologist compares the mean scores of the students on the two tests. Which *t* test should the psychologist use to determine whether there is a significant difference between the two sets of IQ scores? Explain.

10.17. The principal of Jefferson school wishes to determine whether there are differences between teachers and parents in their attitude toward school. At the beginning of the school year, the principal asks 30 randomly selected parents and 28 teachers to complete a 40-item questionnaire designed to measure attitudes toward school. The results are displayed in Table 10.17:

Table 10.17. *t* Test Comparing the Attitudes toward School of Parents and Teachers

Group	n	Mean	SD	t	p
Parents	30	18.30	9.85		
				1.92	.03
Teachers	28	23.07	9.07		

a. Which *t* test should the principal use to compare the responses of the parents and the teachers? Explain.

b. What are the degrees of freedom (*df*)?

c. What are the conclusions of the principal based on the results in the table? Explain.

10.18. The faculty of a local college of education wanted to increase incoming education students' interest and knowledge about STEM (Science, Technology, Engineering, and Mathematics) education and programs. During their first term in the college of education, students learn about STEM; its conceptual framework, issues addressed in teacher education, and specific initiatives available to them. Students are encouraged to take coursework that will help them incorporate STEM goals as an integral part of their teacher preparation program. Thirty students complete a 20-item survey assessing their attitudes towards STEM curriculum at the beginning and at the end of their first education course. Table 10.18 displays the students' pretest and posttest survey scores:

Table 10.18. *t* Test Comparing Pretest and Posttest Mean Attitude Scores of Students toward STEM (n = 30)

Scores	Mean	SD	t	p
Pretest	10.47	2.825		
			−16.662	<.001
Posttest	17.60	1.589		

a. Which *t* test should be used to analyze the data? Explain.

b. What are the degrees of freedom (*df*)?

c. Based on the results in the table, can the course instructor conclude that the interventions worked? Explain.

10.19. Two third-grade teachers randomly divide last year's second grade students into two groups. One group (group 3.a) includes 32 students and the second one (group 3.b) includes 30 students. After dividing the students, the teachers want to confirm that the two groups are indeed similar. They hypothesize that there is no statistically significant difference between the two groups. To compare the two groups, the teachers use ratings given by the students' second-grade teachers at the end of the previous year. The rating scale ranges from 5 ("excellent student") to 1 ("having great difficulties"). Using these ratings, the teachers conduct a *t* test to determine whether the two groups are similar. The results are presented in Table 10.19.1. The *t* test critical values are listed in Table 10.19.2.

Table 10.19.1. *t* Test Comparing the Ratings Assigned by Teachers to Students in Two Classes

Group	n	Mean	SD	t
3.a	32	3.66	1.31	
				2.008
3.b	30	3.00	1.26	

Table 10.19.2. *t* Test Critical Values for Two-Tailed Test for df=60

df	p = .05	p = .02	p = .01
60	2.000	2.390	2.660

a. Which *t* test was used and why?

b. Were the results statistically significant? (See Table 10.19.2.) Explain.

c. What are the teachers' conclusions? Explain.

10.20. A high-school teacher teaching a senior level English Advance Placement (AP) class with 23 students wants to know whether the scores of his students on the verbal portion of the SAT are higher than the scores of other college-bound students in the school. The mean score obtained by the AP English students on the verbal portion of the SAT is 635.13 and the mean score of *all* 678 college-bound seniors in the school on the same test is 430 ($\mu = 430$). A *t* test is used to compare the SAT Verbal scores of the AP English students to the mean score of the college-bound seniors in the school. The results of the *t* test are:

$$\bar{X} = 635.13 \qquad S^2 = 71.53$$
$$t \text{ value} = 13.75 \qquad p = .0001$$

a. Which *t* test is used and why?

b. What are the teacher's conclusions? Explain.

CHAPTER 10 ANSWERS

(10.1)   mean. (Explanation: Since *t* test is used to compare two means, the sample mean is compared to the populations' mean.)

(10.2)   *df* = 44. (Explanation: The number of people in the group minus 1.)

(10.3)   65. (Explanation: The degrees of freedom are computed as: $df = (n_1 - 1) + (n_2 - 1) = 31 + 34 = 65$.)

(10.4)   independent samples. (Explanation: The two groups are independent of each other.)

(10.5)   a single sample. (Explanation: The eighth graders comprise a sample that is compared to the population of students in the state.)

(10.6)   paired. (Explanation: The scores on the two forms are paired because they were obtained by the same students.)

(10.7)   the same as. (Explanation: Only people for whom both pretest and posttest scores are available can participate in the study.)

(10.8)   independent samples. (Explanation: The two genders are independent of each other.)

(10.9)   one-tailed test. (Explanation: Directional hypotheses predict the direction of the outcomes; therefore, a one-tailed test should be used.)

(10.10) two-tailed test. (Explanation: This alternative hypothesis is stated as a null; therefore, a two-tailed test should be used.)

(10.11) more. (Explanation: The two *heterogeneous* groups are likely to overlap more than the two *homogeneous* groups. Therefore, a difference of 4 points between the homogeneous groups is likely to be more statistically significant.)

(10.12) less. (Explanation: A difference of 3 points out of 100 points is proportionally smaller than a difference of 3 points out of 30 points.)

(10.13) The means of the two groups, the variances of the two groups, and the number of people in both groups.

(10.14) a. nondirectional.

           b. null.

           c. directional.

           d. null.

(10.15) Our conclusion is that the experimental treatment is *not* clearly effective. (Explanation: Although the *t* value is statistically significant, a difference of 1 point on a 50-item test probably does not indicate real differences between the two groups. Based on these results alone, we should not conclude that the intervention is effective.)

(10.16) A *t* test for paired samples. (Explanation: The two IQ scores that are gathered for each student are paired; therefore, a paired-samples *t* test should be used.)

(10.17) a. A *t* test for independent samples, because the two groups (parents and teachers) are independent of each other.

           b. *df* = 56 (30 + 28 − 2 = 58 − 2 = 56).

           c. The teachers' mean attitudes toward school was significantly ($p = .03$) more positive (a higher mean) than that of the parents, and slightly more uniform (a lower SD).

(10.18) a. The paired samples *t* test should be used, because the pretest and posttest survey scores were gathered for the same group of education students.

           b. *df* = 29 (30 − 1 = 29).

           c. The course instructor can conclude that the intervention programs to increase education students' interest and knowledge about STEM curriculum were effective, because the survey mean posttest of 17.60

was significantly higher ($p < .001$) than the pretest mean of 10.47. Additionally, the posttest SD of 1.589 on the survey was lower than the pretest SD of 2.825, indicating less variability in students' attitudes towards STEM after the intervention programs.

(**10.19**) a. A *t* test for independent samples, because the two classrooms are independent of each other.

b. Yes. the obtained *t* value of 2.008 exceeds the critical value of 2.000 under $p = .05$. However, there is a very small different between the obtained and critical values.

c. There is a difference of 0.66 points between the means of the two randomly selected groups. The mean score of group 3.a is 3.66; it is higher than the mean of group 3.b, which is 3.00. This difference is statistically significant at $p < .05$. The standard deviations of the two groups are approximately the same.

(**10.20**) a. A *t* test for a single sample, because the mean score of the AP class (the sample) is compared to μ, the mean of the population. (The other college-bound seniors in the school are considered the population.)

b. The difference between the mean score of the AP students and the mean score of the other college-bound students is 205.13 points ($635.13 - 430 = 205.13$). There is a *very* slight chance ($p = .0001$) that this difference could have been obtained by chance alone. The teacher can be quite confident in the conclusion that the AP English students score higher than the rest of the college-bound seniors in the school.

CHAPTER 10 SUPPLEMENTAL MICROSOFT™ EXCEL EXERCISES

S10.1. Open the file "ISEL.xls"

S10.2. You are interested in investigating the change in students' ISEL reading scores from your fall pretest to your spring posttest.

Write the hypothesized relationship:

a) Null Hypothesis:

b) Alternative Hypothesis:

S10.3. Compute a paired-samples *t* test, comparing *ISEL pre% correct* scores to *ISEL post% correct* scores for Snapshots 1–4 (columns FG, JK, NO, RS). Complete the following table:

Snapshot 1	Pretest mean:	_____	Posttest mean:	_____
	Pretest SD:	_____	Posttest SD:	_____
	n:	_____		
	t-value:	_____	*p*-value:	_____
Snapshot 2	Pretest mean:	_____	Posttest mean:	_____
	Pretest SD:	_____	Posttest SD:	_____
	n:	_____		
	t-value:	_____	*p*-value:	_____
Snapshot 3	Pretest mean:	_____	Posttest mean:	_____
	Pretest SD:	_____	Posttest SD:	_____
	n:	_____		
	t-value:	_____	*p*-value:	_____
Snapshot 4	Pretest mean:	_____	Posttest mean:	_____
	Pretest SD:	_____	Posttest SD:	_____
	n:	_____		
	t-value:	_____	*p*-value:	_____

S10.4. Are these one-tail or two-tail significance tests? Explain.

S10.5. Describe the gain from Pretest to Posttest for each of the Snapshots.

S10.6. Using data from the table you completed in S10.3, first create a new table in Excel with 4 columns (Snapshots 1–4) and two rows (Pretest Mean, Posttest Mean). Now create a clustered bar graph for your new table that displays the changes from pretest to posttest for the four snapshots.

CHAPTER 10 ANSWERS FOR MICROSOFT™ EXCEL EXERCISES

(S10.2) a) Null Hypothesis: Fall ISEL Reading scores = Spring ISEL Reading scores OR there is no significant difference between the fall and spring ISEL reading scores.

b) Alternative Hypothesis: Fall ISEL Reading Scores < Spring ISEL Reading Scores OR Fall ISEL Reading Scores are significantly lower than Spring ISEL Reading Scores.

(S10.3)

t test: Paired Two Sample for Means

	Pre %1	Post %1	Pre %2	Post %2	Pre %3	Post %3	Pre %4	Post %4
Mean	75.53	97.48	68.2698	86.86	65.4667	90.733	61.48	93.37
Var	868.10	63.79	357.12	179.94	776.71	274.37	1087.9	231.3
Obs	300	300	300	300	300	300	300	300
Pears Corr.	0.5537		0.691		0.5476		0.59	
Hyp Mean Diff	0		0		0		0	
df	299		299		299		299	
t Stat	−14.67		−23.56		−18.75		−20.5	
P(T<=t) one-tail	2.22E-37		2.05E-70		1.16E-52		3.04E-59	
t Crit One-tail	1.64996		1.64996		1.64996		1.64996	
P(T<=t) two-tail	4.4E-37		4.1E-70		2.3E-52		6.1E-59	
t Crit Two-tail	1.96793		1.96793		1.96793		1.96793	

t test results for Snapshot 1   *t* test results for Snapshot 2   *t* test results for Snapshot 3   *t* test results for Snapshot 4

*Note: Decimals have been rounded.

Snapshot 1	Pretest mean:	75.53	Posttest mean:	97.48
	Pretest SD:	29.46	Posttest SD:	7.99
	n:	300		
	t-value:	−14.67	*p*-value:	.00001
Snapshot 2	Pretest mean:	68.27	Posttest mean:	86.86
	Pretest SD:	18.9	Posttest SD:	13.4
	n:	300		
	t-value:	−23.56	*p*-value:	.00001
Snapshot 3	Pretest mean:	65.47	Posttest mean:	90.73
	Pretest SD:	27.87	Posttest SD:	16.56
	n:	300		
	t-value:	−18.74	*p*-value:	.00001
Snapshot 4	Pretest mean:	61.48	Posttest mean:	93.37
	Pretest SD:	37.99	Posttest SD:	15.21
	n:	300		
	t-value:	−20.50	*p*-value:	.00001

All gains from pretest to posttest are statistically significant. Note the differences in standard deviations between Pretest and Posttest for each snapshot. The scores are more similar for the posttest as indicated by the smaller standard deviation.

(S10.4) They are one-tail tests because we are predicting the direction of the outcome stating that the pretest < posttest, not merely that they are unequal.

(S10.5) The pretests are significantly lower than posttests for all four snapshots. (Note that the table presents the *p*-value for Snapshot 1–4 using an "E" which represents the scientific notation for the digit calculated. It is standard to substitute this notation as $p < .0001$).

(S10.6)

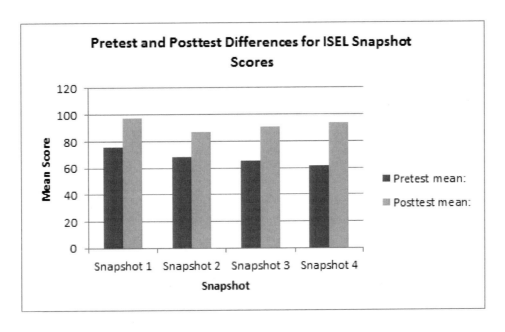

11

Analysis of Variance (ANOVA)

Fill in the blanks:

11.1. While a *t* test is used to compare *two* means, the one-way ANOVA can be used to simultaneously compare _____ groups.

11.2. An ANOVA is considered to be an extension of the *t* test for independent samples because both investigate differences between _____.

11.3. By conducting a one-way ANOVA test to compare multiple (more than 2) group means *simultaneously* instead of conducting a series of *t* tests to compare these means, the potential level of _____ is reduced.

11.4. In order to apply the ANOVA test, the data should be measured on a(n) _____ or _____ scale.

11.5. The one-way ANOVA is used when there is/are _____ independent variable(s).

11.6. With 3 groups, the null hypothesis (H_o) in ANOVA is _____.

11.7. The *total* (or *grand*) mean in ANOVA can be thought of as the mean of _____.

11.8. The SS_W (*within-groups* sum of squares) and the SS_B (*between-groups* sum of squares) are equal to the _____ sum of squares.

11.9. To find the MS_B we divide the SS_B by _____.

11.10. To compute the *F* ratio, we divide the _____ mean square by the _____ mean square.

11.11. Factorial ANOVA is commonly used when there are at least _____ independent variables.

Circle the correct answer between the choices in bold:

11.12. The following is an example of a(n) **null / alternative** hypothesis in ANOVA:

$$\mu_1 \neq \mu_2 \quad \text{and/or} \quad \mu_1 \neq \mu_3 \quad \text{and/or} \quad \mu_2 \neq \mu_3$$

11.13. Post hoc comparisons should be conducted in cases where the *F* ratio **is / is not** statistically significant.

11.14. The *F* ratio is likely to be statistically significant when the differences between the group means are **small / large**.

11.15. The *F* ratio is more likely to be statistically significant when it is used to analyze scores from groups that are **homogeneous / heterogeneous** in regard to the characteristic or behavior being measured.

Answer the following questions:

11.16. Students in three high schools in the district took a geography test. Their test scores were compared using one-way ANOVA. The results of the analysis are shown in Tables 11.16.1 and 11.16.2.

Table 11.16.1. Means and Standard Deviations of Three High School Classes on a Geography Test

School	N	Mean Geography Score	Standard Deviation
A	29	40.83	6.990
B	31	36.29	7.006
C	29	39.21	5.912
TOTAL	89	38.72	6.857

Table 11.16.2. One-Way ANOVA Summary Table Comparing Geography Test Scores of Three High School Classes

	Sum of Squares	df	Mean Square	F	Sig.
Between Groups	318.694	2	159.347	3.588	.032
Within Groups	3819.284	86	44.410		
Total	4137.978	88			

a. Was there a difference in the mean scores of the students in the three schools? Explain.

b. Was there a *statistically significant* difference among the three schools? Explain your conclusions.

c. What is the relationship between the *F* ratio and the two values in the Mean Square column in Table 11.16.2? Explain.

11.17. Three sixth-grade classes in one school (School A) took the same reading test as did 3 other sixth-grade classes in another school (School B). Following are the means and standard deviations obtained by the 3 sixth-grade classes in each of the two schools:

Table 11.17. Means of Three 6th-grade Classes on Reading Tests

SCHOOL	Means		
	6th Grade A	6th Grade B	6th Grade C
School A	50.2	52.8	53.3
School B	41.0	48.5	55.9

Two *separate* one-way ANOVA procedures are conducted to test whether the differences between the three means of the three sixth-grade classes in each of the two schools are statistically significant. *Estimate* which *F* ratio would be larger: The one resulting from analyzing the test scores obtained from the three groups in School A or the one from analyzing the test scores obtained by the three groups in School B. Explain your answer.

11.18. Each of the two figures below (Figure A and Figure B) depicts a set of 3 distributions. Two *separate* one-way ANOVA analyses are performed to test whether there are statistically significant differences between the three means in each school and two *F* ratios are computed. Estimate which of the two *F* ratios is likely to be higher and explain your answer.

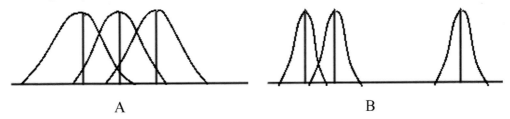

A   B

11.19. Match the interaction shown in the following graph with one of the three *F* ratios (a, b, or c) that was calculated for the interaction. Explain your answer.

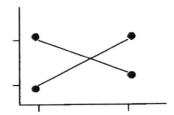

a. $F = 3.23$ ($p = .07$)
b. $F = 5.86$ ($p = .002$)
c. $F = 2.90$ ($p = .09$)

11.20. A pilot-test study comparing two science textbooks was conducted in two schools (School A and School B). In each of the two schools, one fifth-grade class used one science textbook and the other fifth-grade class used the other science textbook. At the end of the year, all students took a standardized test in science. Following is a table listing the mean scores of the two fifth-grade classes in each of the two schools (those that used Textbook 1 and those that used Textbook 2). Study the data in the table. (*Note: Do not attempt to compute the F ratios or the exact level of significance in order to answer the questions below.*)

Table 11.20. **Means of Science Test Scores of 5th-grade Students in Schools A and B Using Textbooks 1 and 2**

School	Mean of 5th-Grade Students Using Textbook 1	Mean of 5th-Grade Students Using Textbook 2
School A	55	53
School B	50	48

a. Are there differences in test scores as a result of using the two textbooks? Explain.
b. Are there differences in performance on the science test between the two schools? Explain.
c. Graph the interaction. Is there an interaction effect? Explain.

CHAPTER 11 ANSWERS

(11.1)   two or more.

(11.2)   the means of independent samples.

(11.3)   error.

(11.4)   interval; ratio.

(11.5)   one.

(11.6) $H_o: \mu_1 = \mu_2 = \mu_3$.

(11.7)   all the scores, from all the groups, combined.

(11.8)   total (i.e., SS_T).

(11.9) df_B (i.e., the degrees of freedom for *between groups*).

(11.10) *between-groups; within-groups.*

(11.11) two.

(11.12) alternative.

(11.13) is.

(11.14) large.

(11.15) homogeneous.

(11.16) a. The students in School A scored the highest (mean of 40.83), followed by students in School C (mean of 39.21). Students in School B scored the lowest (a mean of 36.29).

       b. Yes; the *p* value was .032, which is less than *p* = .05; these results are considered statistically significant (at *p* = .032, or *p* < .05).

       c. In order to calculate the *F* ratio, MS for *Between Groups* is divided by *MS* for *Within Groups*:

$$F = \frac{159.347}{44.410} = 3.588$$

(11.17) From School B, because the differences between the means of the 3 sixth-grade classes in School B (means of 41.0, 48.5, and 55.9) are *larger* than the differences between the means of the 3 sixth-grade classes in School A (means of 50.2, 52.8, and 53.3).

(11.18) The set of distributions in Figure B. The 3 means in Figure B are farther apart from each other compared with the 3 means in Figure A (especially the mean on the right-hand side). Additionally, the 3 groups in Figure A overlap more than the 3 groups in Figure B indicating higher variability of the groups in Figure A. Therefore, an ANOVA analysis of the data depicted in Figure B is likely to result in a higher *F* ratio compared with Figure A.

(11.19) b. (*F* = 5.86). The graph shows a significant interaction and the only *F* ratio that is statistically significant (*p* value of .05 or lower) is the *F* ratio in option b that is listed as *p* = .002.

(11.20) a. Yes; the students in both schools scored higher with Textbook 1.

       b. The students in School A scored higher than the students in School B when using Textbook 1 *and* Textbook 2.

       c. A graph of the interaction would show that the two lines are parallel and there is no interaction effect.

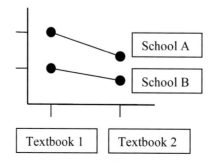

CHAPTER 11 SUPPLEMENTAL MICROSOFT™ EXCEL EXERCISES

Tech Tip

To compute a one-way ANOVA, select "ANOVA: single factor" from the Data-Analysis dialog box under "Tools" menu.

Check the "columns" option in the dialog box to indicate that data are grouped in columns.

S11.1. Open your "ITBS_ANOVA.xls" datafile.

S11.2. Investigate whether there are differences between three groups participating in a Reading intervention: the comparison group, the group in the first year of the intervention, and the group in the second year of the intervention. Generate an ANOVA to compare the differences in the three means of the groups on the ITBS Reading scale score.

Interpreting your ANOVA results:

S11.3. Complete the table based on results from your Excel analyses.

Anova: Single Factor

SUMMARY

Groups	Count	Sum	Ave	Variance
Comparison Class READING (S.S.)				
1st Yr Implementation Class READING (S.S.)				
2nd Yr Implementation Class READING (S.S.)				

ANOVA

Source of Variation	SS	df	MS	F	P-value	F crit
Between Groups						
Within Groups						
Total						

S11.4. How many groups are in your analysis?

S11.5. How many students are in each group?

S11.6. Report the *F* value and *p* value. What do they indicate about the statistical significance of the test?

S11.7. Since Excel does not provide post hoc comparison tests, how might you use *t*-tests to test for significant differences?

S.11.8. Look at the means and identify the groups scoring the highest and the lowest. How can educators look at the *practical difference* between the three means and speculate as to the effectiveness of the intervention?

CHAPTER 11 ANSWERS FOR MICROSOFT™ EXCEL EXERCISES

(S11.3)

Anova: Single Factor

SUMMARY

Groups	Count	Sum	Ave	Variance
Comparison Class READING (S.S.)	97	12553	129.4124	157.4532
1st Yr Imp Class READING (S.S.)	97	15064	155.299	135.6701
2nd Yr Imp Class READING (S.S.)	97	17164	176.9485	427.9661

ANOVA

Source of Variation	SS	df	MS	F	P-value	F crit
Between Groups	109884.7	2	54942.34	228.5806	3.54E-60	3.027111
Within Groups	69224.58	288	240.3631			
Total	179109.3	290				

(S11.4) There are three groups in the analysis: a comparison group, a first year group, and a Second year group.

(S11.5) Comparison group $n = 97$, First year group $n = 97$, and second year group $n = 97$.

(S11.6) $F = 228.5806$, $p < .00001$. The three groups are significantly different from each other. In fact, the obtained value is a very large F ratio that indicates large between-group differences for the three groups. (Note that the table presents the p-value as the scientific notation 3.54E-60, indicating that the decimal precedes *60* "zeros" before 3.54. It is standard to substitute this notation as $p < .0001$.)

(S11.7) You can conduct a t-test for each pairwise comparison (i.e., Comparison vs. First year, Comparison vs. Second year, and First year vs. Second year).

(S11.8) Looking at the scores, the Second Year reading scores for the intervention group are the highest. Educators can use their experiences with "typical" class reading averages to make judgments about whether the difference between the means of 129, 155, and 177 are *practically important*.

12

Chi Square

Fill in the blanks:

12.1.   In a chi square test, the *observed* frequencies are compared to the _____ frequencies.

12.2.   The null hypothesis for the chi square test states that there is no statistically significant difference between the _____ frequencies and the _____ frequencies.

12.3.   In order to use a chi square test, the data have to be in the form of _____.

12.4.   In order to create categories for a chi square test, observations that are measured on an interval scale should first be divided into categories in a _____ way.

12.5.   The degrees of freedom (*df*) for a 3×4 chi square table are _____.

12.6.   In a *goodness of fit* chi square test with 4 cells, the degrees of freedom (*df*) are _____.

Circle the correct answer between the choices in bold:

12.7.   A chi square test is called a *test of independence* when there is(are) **one / two** variables(s).

12.8.   The chi square value increases as the differences between the *observed* and *expected* frequencies **increase / decrease**.

12.9.   In a 2×2 chi square test the total number of frequencies in the first row **should always be the same as / may be different than** the total number of frequencies in the second row.

For each of the following examples, choose which type of chi square test should be used: *Goodness of fit test,* or *test of independence:*

12.10. To test whether a four-sided spinning top has an equal probability of landing on any of its four sides the chi square _____ should be used.

12.11. To test whether two variables are related to or are independent of each other the chi square _____ should be used.

12.12. To test whether there are differences or similarities between girls and boys in the type of books (e.g., fiction, sci-fi) they read the chi square _____ should be used.

12.13. To test whether the number of right- and left-handed students in a given school is higher than the national proportions the chi square _____ should be used.

Answer/compute the following questions:

12.14. A random sample of 100 men and 100 women were asked whether they would be willing to work as unpaid volunteers. The results indicate that 64% of the women and 54% of the men responded YES to this question, while 36% of the women and 46% of the men responded NO to the question. The observed and expected frequencies are displayed in Table 12.14 below. The chi square test was used to determine whether the women and men in the study differ in their willingness to work as unpaid volunteers. The obtained chi square value was 2.067 ($\chi^2_{(obt)}$ = 2.06). The appropriate critical value at p = .05 is 3.841 ($\chi^2_{crit\,(.05)}$ = 3.841).

Table 12.14. Chi Square Table Showing the Observed and Expected Frequencies of Responses by Gender to the Question: Are You Willing to Work as an Unpaid Volunteer?

Group	Yes Observed	Yes Expected	No Observed	No Expected	Total
Women	64	59	36	41	100
Men	54	59	46	41	100

a. Which chi square test was used to analyze the data and determine whether there are gender differences between the responses of the men and women who participated in the survey? Explain.

b. What was the null hypothesis for the study?

c. Was there a statistically significant gender difference between the responses of the male and female participants? Explain.

12.15. Undergraduate students in a large state university are required to take an introduction to psychology course. Three sections of this course are offered at the same time and are taught by three different instructors. The chi square test is used to determine if any of these sections has significantly more students, which may indicate that the instructor of that section is more popular than the other two instructors. The enrollment figures for the three sections are presented in the following table. The obtained chi square value is 6.29 (χ^2 = 6.29) significant at the p < .05 level.

Table 12.15. A Comparison of the Numbers of Students Enrolled in Three Sections of the Course Introduction to Psychology

Instructor	Number of Students Enrolled
Dr. Smith	114
Dr. Brown	128
Dr. Johnson	91

a. Which chi square test should be used to determine whether any of the sections has a statistically significantly higher number of students? Explain.

b. What are the *expected* frequencies?

c. What are the degrees of freedom (*df*)?

d. What are your conclusions? Explain.

12.16. Randomly selected groups of 120 parents and 150 teachers from one school district are surveyed about their attitudes toward inclusion. One of the questions asks them whether they oppose or support inclusions and their responses to this question are recorded in Table 12.16. The data were analyzed using a chi square test. The obtained chi square value is 5.65, significant at the .02 level ($p = .02$).

Table 12.16. A Comparison of the Attitudes of Parents and Teachers toward Inclusion

Group	Support	Oppose	Total
Parent	75	45	120
Teachers	72	78	150

a. Which chi square test should be used to analyze the data and answer the research questions? Explain.

b. Is there a statistically significant difference in the responses of the parents and teachers? Explain.

12.17. In a recent national poll, people were asked the following question: "In your opinion, how important is it to improve the nation's inner-city schools?" The responses of city residents who do not have school-age children were compared to the national responses. A chi square test was used to analyze the data in order to determine whether there is a difference in responses between those who live in cities and do not have school-age children and the national responses. The results of the study are displayed in Table 12.17. The analysis revealed a chi square value of 4.32, significant at $p = .36$.

Table 12.17. A Comparison of the Responses of City Residents without School-Age Children and the Responses of a National Sample to the Question: "In your opinion, how important is it to improve the nation's inner-city schools?"

Response	No Children in School	National Totals
Very Important	78	80
Fairly Important	13	15
Not Very Important	6	3
Not Important at All	2	1
Don't Know	1	1

a. Which chi square test was used to analyze the data? Explain.

b. What was the null hypothesis?

c. What are the conclusions of the study? Explain.

12.18. A psychologist studying young children is interested in the development of color preferences among pre-school boys. The psychologist hypothesizes that the boys would prefer certain colors to others. For the purpose of the study, only five primary colors are included: yellow, red, blue, green, and black. A group of 50 preschool boys are brought to a room and are asked to select one ball from a box full of balls. In the box there are 50 yellow balls, 50 red, 50 blue, 50 green, and 50 black. The colors of the balls chosen by the boys are recorded and a chi square test is used to analyze the data and answer the psychologist's research question. The obtained chi square value is 8.800 ($\chi^2_{obt} = 8.800$) and the appropriate critical value at $p = .05$ is 9.488 ($\chi^2_{crit\,(.05,4)} = 9.488$). Following are the colors chosen by the boys (Table 12.18):

Table 12.18. A Distribution of Colors Chosen by 50 Preschool Boys

Color	No. of Times the Color Was Chosen (Observed Frequencies)
Yellow	6
Red	12
Blue	14
Green	4
Black	14

a. Which chi square test was used to analyze the data? Explain.

b. What are the expected frequencies?

c. What are the study's conclusions? Explain.

CHAPTER 12 ANSWERS

(12.1) expected.

(12.2) observed; expected (or: expected; observed).

(12.3) frequencies.

(12.4) logical or defensible.

(12.5) 6. (Explanation: In chi square test of independence, the df are computed as:[#Rows − 1] × [#Columns − 1]. In this example it is: [3 − 1] × [4 − 1] = 6.)

(12.6) 3. (Explanation: The degrees of freedom are computed by subtracting 1 from the number of cells. In this example, the df are: 4 − 1 = 3.)

(12.7) two. (Explanation: Chi square test of independence is conducted to determine whether the two factors [independent variables] are independent of each other.)

(12.8) increase. (Explanation: Chi square is conducted to compare observed to expected frequencies. The difference between observed and expected frequencies is the numerator in the equation to compute the chi square value; therefore, the higher the numerator, the higher the chi square value.)

(12.9) may be different than. (Explanation: Because the chi square test is used to study proportions, the total numbers of observed frequencies in the two rows do not have to be exactly the same.)

(12.10) *goodness of fit test* (with equal-probability expected frequencies). (Explanation: This is similar to the example of testing a coin in chapter 12.)

(12.11) *test of independence.* (Explanation: When there are two variables, we use the test of independence.)

(12.12) *test of independence.* (Explanation: This is a test of independence because there are two independent variables: gender and the type of book chosen.)

(12.13) *goodness of fit test* (with unequal expected frequencies). (Explanation: The number of right-handed and left-handed children in the school is the *observed* frequencies and the national norms comprise the *expected* frequencies. We do not assume that the number of right-handed children in the population is the same as the number of left-handed children.)

(12.14) a. A 2 × 2 chi square *test of independence.* (Explanation: There were two independent variables [gender and the response choices], each with two levels [two genders and two response choices]).

b. The null hypothesis stated that there was no significant difference between the men and women in the study in their willingness to work as unpaid volunteers.

c. The obtained chi square value of 2.06 (χ^2_{obt} = 2.06) *does not* exceed the critical value of 3.841 at the p = .05 level ($\chi^2_{crit (.05)}$ = 3.841). Therefore, we *retain* the null hypothesis. The majority of the respondents in both groups indicated that they would be willing to work as unpaid volunteers. Although more women than men were willing to volunteer, the difference between the responses of the two genders is not *statistically* significant.

(12.15) a. A *goodness of fit* chi square test with *equal* expected frequencies. (Explanation: The null hypothesis is that the number of students enrolled in each of the three sections would be the same.)

b. The expected frequencies are 111, 111, 111. (Explanation: Start by finding the total number of students, which is 333. To find the expected frequencies in each cell, divide the total number by 3.)

c. df = 2. (Explanation: the degrees of freedom are the number of cells minus 1.)

d. The null hypothesis that states that there is no statistically significant difference in the numbers of students enrolled in each section is rejected ($p < .05$) in favor of the alternative hypothesis that states that there is a significant difference in the number of students enrolled in the three sections. Specifically, Dr. Brown is the most popular instructor and Dr. Johnson is the least popular instructor.

(12.16) a. The chi square *test of independence* should be used. (Explanation: There are two independent variables—groups and responses).

b. We can conclude that the difference between the parents and the teachers is statistically significant at $p = .02$ (or $p < .05$). We reject the null hypothesis that states that there are no differences between the two groups. The likelihood that the decision to reject the null hypothesis is the wrong decision is 2%. The results of the survey show that the majority of the parents (63%) support inclusion while the opinions of the teachers are almost evenly divided (52% oppose and 48% support).

(12.17) a. A *goodness of fit* chi square test for one variable with *unequal* expected frequencies. The responses of those without children are viewed as the sample, and they are compared to a larger population (the expected frequencies) that contains *all* the respondents.

b. The null hypothesis stated that there are no differences between the responses of city residents without school-age children and the responses obtained for the population at large.

c. We retain the null hypothesis. Although the responses of the two groups are not exactly the same, the observed differences are probably due to chance alone and not because of real differences in opinions between the groups.

(12.18) a. A *goodness of fit* chi square test with equal expected frequencies. (Explanation: There is one independent variable—the colors of the balls—and we expect all the balls to be equally chosen.)

b. The expected frequencies are 10. (Explanation: To find the expected frequencies, divide the number of boys [which is 50] by 5 [the number of colors in the study]).

c. The table reveals that there are differences in color preferences; black and blue are the most popular colors, followed closely by red; green is the least popular color. While the differences between the 5 colors *seem* quite large, they are not *statistically significant* and could have happened by chance more than 5% of the time. The obtained chi square value of 8.800 is lower than the appropriate critical value of 9.488 (at the $p = .05$ level). Therefore, we *retain* the null hypothesis. (Actually, according to the computer printout, the exact p value is .07 [which is close to $p = .05$]. With a larger sample size it is likely that there would be statistically significant differences in the color choices.)

13

Reliability

Circle the correct answer between the choices in bold:

13.1.   Instruments measuring human behavior tend to be **more / less** reliable than those measuring physical characteristics.

13.2.   The reliability of achievement tests is likely to be **higher / lower** than that of tests measuring attitudes and opinions.

13.3.   The reliability of a test is likely to *increase* when the test's error component is **increased / decreased**.

13.4.   One way to *increase* the test's reliability is to **increase / decrease** the number of items in the test.

13.5.   To assess the reliability of a test using *internal consistency* methods, the test is administered **one time / multiple times**.

13.6.   To assess the inter-scorer reliability of an essay, the degree of **agreement / differences** between people who score the same essay is commonly used.

13.7.   The higher the reliability, the **lower / higher** the standard error of measurement (SEM).

13.8.   When the majority of the items on a test are *too easy* or *too difficult*, the test's reliability is likely to **increase / decrease**.

13.9.   Teacher-made tests are likely to be **more / less** reliable than commercially produced tests.

13.10. The reliability of tests used for decisions about individual students should be **higher / lower** than the reliability of tests used for group decisions.

Circle the best answer:

13.11. Obtaining similar scores for the same group of people from repeatedly using the same instrument over and over is used as an indication of the instrument's _____

    a. standard error of measurement.
    b. test norms.
    c. reliability.

13.12. Tests that are highly reliable are likely to have standard error of measurements (SEMs) that are _____ in similar tests with low reliability.

    a. lower than
    b. higher than
    c. the same as

13.13. When we administer a second time the same test to the same group of people and correlate the results, we are using the _____ approach to assessing the test reliability.

    a. alternate forms
    b. internal consistency
    c. split half
    d. test-retest

13.14. When a student has a score of 85 on a standardized test and the test has a standard error of measurement (SEM) of 5, it means that the student's true score is expected to be between 80 and 90 _____% of the time.

    a. 50
    b. 68
    c. 95
    d. 100

Answer the following question:

13.15. A Spanish teacher is using a new instructional unit that he developed that includes songs, dances, and video clips. The teacher wants to assess his students' opinions towards this new unit. He develops a 15-item survey that measures students' attitudes. Each item has 4 response choices: Strongly Agree (4 points); Agree (3 points); Disagree (2 points) and Strongly Disagree (1 point). After administering the survey once to the students, the teacher wants to assess the survey's reliability. What method should the teacher use to assess the survey's reliability and why?

CHAPTER 13 ANSWERS

(13.1)   less. (Explanation: Physical characteristics tend to be more stable than human behavior.)

(13.2)   higher. (Explanation: Tests that measure achievement provide more consistent and stable information; therefore, they are more reliable than tests that measure attitudes and behavior that tend to fluctuate.)

(13.3)   decreased. (Explanation: Tests with smaller error components are likely to be more reliable.)

(13.4)   increase. (Explanation: All things being equal, a longer test is more reliable than a shorter test.)

(13.5)   one time. (Explanation: Unlike most other approaches to assess reliability, internal consistency methods can be applied using scores from a single testing.)

(13.6)   agreement. (Explanation: The degree [or percent] of agreement between scorers or raters is used as an index of reliability.)

(13.7)   lower. (Explanation: The standard error of measurement [SEM] is an index of the level of *error* in a test; therefore, a more reliable test has a smaller level of error.)

(13.8)   decrease. (Explanation: Tests are most reliable when the items have an average level of difficulty.)

(13.9)   less. (Explanation: Commercially produced tests are written by professionals and undergo extensive review and analysis prior to being administered on a large scale, whereas teachers may not have the expertise or the time necessary to design such tests.)

(13.10) higher. (Explanation: The stakes are higher when decisions are made about individuals; therefore, tests that are used to assess individuals should be more reliable than tests used for group decisions.)

(13.11) c. (Explanation: One way to assess reliability is to administer the same test two or more times to the same group of people and correlate the results from these repeated testing sessions.)

(13.12) a. (Explanation: Standard error of measurement is related to reliability, as can be seen from the formula used to compute SEM [see below]. Therefore, the higher the reliability, the lower the SEM.)

$$SEM = SD\sqrt{1 - RELIABILITY}$$

(13.13) d. (Explanation: Test-retest is the only method out of the choices provided that involves repeatedly administering the same test to the same group of people.)

(13.14) b. (Explanation: Because the observed score is 85, SEM is 5, and the range reported for the student's true score is 80–90, we can conclude that this range is within ±1SEM, which corresponds to a confidence level of 68%.)

(13.15) Since the survey was administered only one time, the Spanish teacher would need to use an internal consistency approach to assess the reliability. The items on the survey are scored on a scale of 4–1. Therefore, the teacher cannot use the split-half reliability or the KR 20 and KR 21 approaches, because these approaches assume that items are scored as 1 (correct) or 0 (incorrect). Thus, the Spanish teacher should use Cronbach's coefficient alpha to obtain the internal consistency of the survey, which can be used with any type of items.

14

Validity

Circle the correct answer between the choices in bold:

14.1. Most tests are valid for **a single / multiple** purpose(s).

14.2. When there is a poor match between course content and a test that is used to assess students in the course, the test is likely to have a **high / low** content validity.

14.3. Veteran teachers who are experienced test-writers are expected to write achievement tests for their own classrooms that would have **higher / lower** content validity compared with commercial tests that are designed to be used nationally in a variety of classrooms.

14.4. Well-defined instructional objectives may help teachers write tests that have high **content / construct** validity.

14.5. When a test simply *appears* to measure what it is intended to measure, we conclude that the test has a high **predictive / face** validity.

14.6. When a test systematically discriminates against a group of test-takers, the test is considered to **have a low construct validity / be biased**.

Circle the best answer:

14.7. A high correlation of a newly developed instrument with another well-established instrument *measuring the same thing* indicates a high _____ validity.

   a. content
   b. concurrent
   c. face

14.8.   The type of validity that is most important for *achievement tests* is the _____ validity.

   a. content
   b. face
   c. construct

14.9.   The type of validity that is most important for measuring *psychological traits* is the _____ validity.

   a. face
   b. content
   c. construct

14.10. When a test simply *appears* to measure what it is intended to measure, we conclude that the test has high _____ validity.

   a. predictive
   b construct
   c. face

Answer the following questions:

14.11. A middle school psychologist is interested in the validity of a group IQ test that is used by the school to assess students' aptitudes and cognitive abilities. This group IQ test is included in a norm-referenced achievement test battery that is administered to all sixth-grade students in the district. To determine whether the group IQ test is a valid measure of students' aptitudes, the school psychologist chooses at random 30 sixth-grade students and gives them an individually administered IQ test that is well-known for being a reliable and valid IQ measure.

   a. Which type of validity would be most appropriate to assess in this case? Explain.
   b. What analysis can the psychologist carry out to assess the validity of the *group* IQ test?

14.12. The dean of a medical school wants to assess the relationship between two tests: (a) the MCAT (medical college admission test), which is a nationally administered medical school admission test that all medical students have to take; and (b) the first part of the Medical Board examination, which is administered at the end of the second year in medical school. The dean supports the use of the MCAT as an admission test to predict medical students' performance on the portion of the Medical Board examination that they are required to take at the end of the second year in medical school.

   a. What type of validity should the dean try to obtain regarding the MCAT? Explain.
   b. How can the dean assess this type of validity? Explain.

CHAPTER 14 ANSWERS

(14.1) a single. (Explanation: A test can be valid only for one specific purpose for which it was developed.)

(14.2) low. (Explanation: A good match between the test items and the course or unit content validity helps ensure high content validity on achievement tests.)

(14.3) higher. (Explanation: Teachers can write items that more closely match what they have taught in class.)

(14.4) content. (Explanation; Well-defined objectives help guide the teachers by listing the content of the materials taught in class. Teachers can then write test items that correspond to the objectives.)

(14.5) face. (Explanation: Tests that are judged superficially, without further study, as being appropriate for a given purpose are said to have face validity.)

(14.6) be biased. (Explanation: Test bias occurs when the test systematically discriminates against a subgroup of test takers, such as one of the genders or an ethnic group.)

(14.7) b.

(14.8) a.

(14.9) c.

(14.10) c.

(14.11) a. The school psychologist should try to assess the *concurrent* validity of the group IQ test by correlating the individually administered IQ scores obtained by the 30 randomly chosen sixth-grade students to their group IQ scores. The well-established individually administered IQ test would serve as the criterion to which the group IQ test is compared.

b. The school psychologist can correlate the results from the group and individually administered IQ tests for the 30 students for whom both types of IQ scores are available. A high positive correlation would indicate that the two tests measure similar cognitive abilities and aptitudes.

(14.12) a. The dean should try to obtain information about the *predictive* validity of the MCAT in order to decide whether to continue to rely on it to predict students' scores on the Medical Board examination at the end of the second year in medical school.

b. The dean can correlate scores from the MCAT with scores on the Medical Board examination given at the end of the second year in medical school. A high correlation would provide evidence for the predictive validity of the MCAT as a predictor of students' performance on the Medical Board examination that is given at the end of the second year of medical school. Of course, this does not mean that MCAT can predict who would be the best doctor or who will perform well on future medical school examinations; only that those who score high on the MCAT would also do well on the Medical Board examination that is given at the end of the second year to medical students.

Planning and Conducting Research Studies

Circle the correct answer between the choices in bold:

15.1. Research plans for *quantitative* studies are usually **more / less** detailed compared with plans for *qualitative* studies.

15.2. After a study has started, its participants **should / should not** be allowed to withdraw from the study.

15.3. When teachers conduct action research in their classrooms with students they know well, they **should / should not** be concerned about ethical issues.

15.4. Opinions that contradict those of the researcher writing the research report literature review **should / should not** be included in the report.

15.5. A description of how the sample that was used in the study was selected is likely to be found in the **Methodology / Literature Review** chapter.

15.6. *Detailed* information about a standardized test that was used in a study, such as its norms, reliability, and validity, is likely to be found in the **Abstract / Methodology chapter**.

15.7. A very *brief* description of how the present study was conducted is likely to be found in the **Methodology chapter / Abstract**.

15.8. Proposals are usually written in **past / present / future** tense.

15.9. Research reports are usually written in **past / present / future** tense.

15.10. The literature reviews in research *reports* tend to be **shorter / longer** than in research *proposals*.

Circle the best answer:

15.11. Which of the following is NOT included in research proposals?

    a. The study's results.
    b. The study's methodology.
    c. A review of literature related to the study.
    d. Introduction.

15.12. Which document may be viewed as a blueprint for the planned study?

    a. Discussion.
    b. Proposal.
    c. Abstract.
    d. Literature Review.

15.13. The most comprehensive rationale for the study is likely to be found in the _____ chapter.

    a. Methodology
    b. Results
    c. Introduction
    d. Literature Review

15.14. When writing the final research report, the study's limitations should be included in the _____ chapter.

    a. Results
    b. Methodology
    c. Literature Review
    d. Discussion

15.15. When writing a literature review, it should be organized _____

    a. in chronological order.
    b. by topics and subtopics.
    c. as an annotated bibliography.
    d. from the earliest to the latest references.

15.16. The statistical findings of the study are presented *in detail* in the _____

    a. Abstract.
    b. Methodology chapter.
    c. Introduction chapter.
    d. Results chapter.

15.17. Most of the background information, such as summaries of other studies related to the present study, is reported in the study's _____

   a. Literature Review.
   b. Methodology.
   c. Procedure.
   d. Abstract.

15.18. An explanation of some possible reasons why the results of a study that is described in the research report have not confirmed its hypothesis is found in the _____

   a. Study's proposal.
   b. Methodology chapter.
   c. Results chapter.
   d. Discussion chapter.

15.19. In a report on an experimental study, a *detailed* description of the intervention is likely to be found in the _____ section of the *Methodology* chapter.

   a. Instrument
   b. Sample
   c. Procedure
   d. Data Analysis

15.20. The following sentence was included in a research report written by a teacher-researcher: "I believe that additional studies in other settings with more diverse populations should be conducted to explore the relationship between the opinions of parents and students toward sex education." This sentence most likely was included in the report's _____

   a. Appendix.
   b. Sample description section.
   c. Data analysis section.
   d. Discussion (under Suggestions for Further Research).

15.21. The following sentence: "This study will explore three research questions using test data collected in the previous year" is likely to be found in the study's _____

   a. Proposal.
   b. Final Research Report.
   c. Abstract.
   d. Discussion.

15.22. A new fourth-grade teacher wants to understand why some of her students do not complete their homework regularly, even when the amount of work given is minimal. The teacher decides to conduct a study to explore this issue. She plans to survey all 28 students in her class, as well as their parents, the other teachers in the school, and all the school administrators. She prepares a list of 25 questions to be included in the survey about the value of homework and the amount of work involved in completing them regularly. The teacher then submits her plan to the school principal and is a bit surprised by the principal's guarded reaction.

While we encourage teacher action research, we agree with the principal that there are problems with the teacher's proposed research. Make a list of some concerns and potential problems that you see in the teacher's plans and compare them to the list that is included in the answers to this chapter. (The list that is provided is a partial list; other points can be easily added.) Hopefully, you will be able to find at least three problems that are on the list and, perhaps, come up with others that are not on the list!

CHAPTER 15 ANSWERS

(15.1) more. (Explanation: Plans for quantitative research studies tend to be more detailed and not likely to be changed once the study starts whereas qualitative research studies can evolve and be modified after the start of the study.)

(15.2) should. (Explanation: All participants, in all types of studies, should be allowed to withdraw from the study at any time.)

(15.3) should. (Explanation: All researchers, including teachers who study their own classrooms, should be concerned about issues of ethics.)

(15.4) should. (Explanation: The literature review should present a balanced overview of the topic being investigated, including contradicting opinions and findings.)

(15.5) Methodology. (Explanation: Detailed information about the sample should be included in the first part of the *Methodology* chapter.)

(15.6) Methodology chapter. (Explanation: While some brief information about an instrument used in the study may be found in the *Abstract*, detailed information is likely to be found in the study's *Methodology*.)

(15.7) Abstract. (Explanation: Because the *Abstract* is usually limited in length, it can contain only brief information about the study.)

(15.8) future. (Explanation: The proposal describes the future plans of the researcher.)

(15.9) past. (Explanation: The report describes a study that has been concluded; therefore, *past* tense should be used.)

(15.10) longer. (Explanation: Proposals tend to be shorter in general than the full research report and therefore the literature reviews in proposals are also shorter.)

(15.11) a. (Explanation: Proposals are written before the study is conducted; therefore, they do not report the study's results. *Methodology*, *Literature Review*, and *Introduction* can be found in both proposals and research reports.)

(15.12) b. (Explanation: The proposal describes how the proposed study will be carried out; therefore, it is considered the blueprint for the study.)

(15.13) c. (Explanation: The rationale for the study, its significance, and research questions and hypotheses are usually presented in the introduction to the study.)

(15.14) d. (Explanation: The limitations of the study are usually included and acknowledged in the Discussion chapter.)

(15.15) b. (Explanation: The literature review should be a well-organized synthesis of the existing research on the topic of the study.)

(15.16) d. (Explanation: While the *Abstract* is likely to summarize briefly the study's results, a comprehensive description of the results are found in the *Results* chapter.)

(15.17) a. (Explanation: One of the main goals of the *Literature Review* is to provide background information about the topic of the study.)

(15.18) d. (Explanation: Explanations of the study's findings and interpretations of the results are found in the *Discussion* chapter.)

(15.19) c. (Explanation: In all studies, and especially in experimental studies, it is very important to have a clear and detailed description of the data collection procedures and any intervention that was implemented. The details should be specific enough for others to duplicate the study, if they wish to do so.)

(15.20) d. (Explanation: This sentence includes suggestions for future research and, therefore, is likely to be included in the Discussion chapter.)

(15.21) a. (Explanation: Future tense is used, which is typical of a research proposal.)

(15.22) A partial list of potential concerns and problems:

- The teacher should clearly communicate to all involved the purpose of the study, her research questions, and her plans for collecting her data.
- The teacher needs to obtain permissions from all involved before proceeding with data collection. This is especially important when studying students. (You should always check the policies at your own school before undertaking such a study.)
- The teacher should read the literature about the topic of homework before starting with the proposed study and prior to planning the study and creating the survey.
- A timetable should be included. The teacher has to show how she plans to carry out the different phases of the study.
- The survey to be used should be developed before the start of the study. The teacher should pilot test the survey and ask for comments and feedback prior to using it on a large scale.
- The teacher may want to have a shorter survey (less than 25 items) to increase the likelihood that students, parents, colleagues, and administrators will complete the survey.
- The teacher should think about all the logistics involved in administering the surveys; e.g., how to distribute and how to get them back.
- Plans for data entry and analysis should be made and communicated before the start of the study.
- The teacher should explain to the students and their parents that their participation is not mandatory and ask for their help. She should clearly explain to them why she would like to conduct the study.
- The research plan is definitely too ambitious for a new teacher. Scaling down and focusing on what the teacher needs to do first in her job as a new classroom teacher takes priority over her desire to study issues related to students' homework completion.

About the Authors

Ruth Ravid is professor of education at National College of Education, National-Louis University, Illinois. Her areas of interest include teacher research, classroom assessment, and school-university collaborative research. She holds an M.A. and a Ph.D. in education from Northwestern University.

Elizabeth Oyer is the director of EvalSolutions Inc. in Carmel, Indiana. She directs evaluation and web development services throughout the nation for state agencies, universities, and school districts as well as non-profits and businesses. Dr. Oyer holds an M.S. and Ph.D. in educational psychology and inquiry from Indiana University.